# CZECH POINT:
# Keys to Lucrative Property Investment

*Nathan Brown*

CZECH POINT 101 Czech Point: Keys to Lucrative Property
Investment – 2nd Edition Nathan Brown

Copyeditor: Cathy Reed
Cover Design: Giovanni Auriemma
Cover photo: Prague © Michaela Kobyakov / sxc.hu
Interior Design: Iryna Spica

Published in Czech Republic by CZECH POINT 101
ISBN 978-80-905448-0-2

# PREFACE

Everyone's favourite (or not) bombastic personality Donald Trump wrote in his book *Think Like a Billionaire:* 'Real estate is at the core of almost every business, and it's certainly at the core of most people's wealth. In order to build your wealth and improve your business smarts, you need to know about real estate.'

In the interest of enjoying more time at our favourite hobby, or more time with our family, or being able to afford the retirement we would like, we want to use our earned money sagely. For most people, this should include a real estate investment strategy.

Investment property is the top choice not only for many 'uber'-wealthy individuals like Donald Trump but also for hundreds of thousands of ordinary individuals who are able to use it to achieve their goals in life.

● ● ● ● ● ● ● ● ● ● ● ● ● ● ● ● ● ● ● ● ● ● ● ● ● ● ● ● ● ● ● ● ● ● ● ● ● ●

### *Why Czech Republic?*

*My wife and I moved to Czech Republic in 2004 after deciding that if we wanted to experience living in another country it had to be before we had children. Well, one thing led to another and now we have children and live in another country.*

*Investing in property is a family tradition for me. My father introduced me to it at the young age of 22 by helping me invest in a four-plex property. I learned the value of what my dad called 'sweat equity' as we worked to improve the units ourselves to keep the costs down.*

*Since then, our family has continued to jointly invest in property and we currently own 38 rental units, mostly residential.*

*In 2005, I bought CZECH POINT 101 as an existing business in its fledgling stages. Initially the clients were non-Czechs who were trying to do any sort of business in Czech Republic, from setting up a company to getting visas and relocating. Gradually we have turned the company focus exclusively to investment properties and we have many local clients.*

*In the early days it wasn't easy. It took me time to learn the system, build a strong team, and find competent lawyers and accountants.*

*In the meantime, I bought investment property personally in the country, using all the same processes we do with clients. I still continue to invest in Czech properties and am always looking for good opportunities.*

• • • • • • • • • • • • • • • • • • • • • • • • • • • • • • • • • • • •

## THE INS AND OUTS OF CZECH PROPERTY INVESTING

This book will examine the fundamentals and nuances of property investing with a particular focus on the Czech market.

Although the chapters will focus primarily on investment property, much of the material also applies to buying a personal dwelling. In fact, if more individuals would take a business type approach to their personal dwelling, it would help their financial situation considerably. Don't ask my wife for her opinion on this though.

The structure of the book will follow a full property investment life-cycle, right from the decision-making on the purchase side to the sale and exit strategy.

Readers of this book will be at different points in the cycle and so it is possible for you to go directly to those sections of the book which are most applicable to your situation.

## DISCLAIMER

As the author of this book, I will give you an honest disclaimer.

I am a strong proponent of property investing as I have seen the benefits personally. Why? Recently I cashed out a portfolio of mutual funds and bonds that my wife and I owned because over a 10-year period they had provided a compound annual return of only 2.5% (adjusted for inflation).

Our properties, by comparison, had achieved *a minimum* of 15% (also adjusted for inflation) compound annual return for a similar period, even factoring in price decreases through the biggest recession since the 1930s.

From my personal experience, I have seen no investment that returns better than property, as long as a person approaches it in a thoughtful and systematic way.

Also as a disclaimer, I will tell you that I am actively involved in a Czech company which provides many services related to property.

So you could say I have an 'invested interest' in the subject of property and the chapters are biased that way. Let the reader beware.

# ACKNOWLEDGMENTS

I would like to start by thanking all those who assisted in making this book possible. First and foremost are my Dad and Mom who worked hard to help each of their children (all six of us) get the best start in life, not only in money matters but also emotionally, morally and spiritually. As a parent myself now, I understand how much work this involves. And thank you to my dear wife who has been a steadfast and supportive partner living a long way from 'home' for many years.

I especially thank members of our CZECH POINT 101 team who contributed parts of this book and were a constant source of feedback and assistance. They include JUDr. Daniel Burget, Khup Gin Khan, Karel and Bc. Edita Kohoutek, Pavel Pařízek, Jan Palán, Tereza Lukuvkova and Bc. Tomáš Repaský. Without having such a good team, I would never have been able to take myself away from the day-to-day activities of a business and devote so much time to writing a book.

Thanks also to the kindness of those who assisted with suggestions and editing, including Jo Miller, Simon Rollason, James Tomlin, Mark Norris, James Prior, Daniel Peacock, Christopher Lean and Silvia Preda.

# TABLE OF CONTENTS

# WEIGHING
# THE DECISION

## Chapter One

# TWO AREAS WHERE INVESTING IN PROPERTY WALLOPS THE ALTERNATIVES

A downturn in any financial market can prompt even the most zealous aficionado to re-examine why they are involved in that particular investment vehicle.

In the next chapter, we will discuss the *disadvantages* of investing in real estate because, yes, there are some; but for this chapter, let's look at the top two reasons why it beats alternatives.

### 1. Leverage

What is leverage? In one simple sentence, you could say it is doing more with less.

An example of leverage is students borrowing money in order to complete an education which will ultimately pay them back in the future with increased earnings.

Leverage in real estate is typically achieved by borrowing money from banks up to a certain percentage of the total price of the property.

Leverage will amplify the results of your investment either up or down.

A demonstration of confidence that real estate typically goes up in price is that a bank would never lend you money at 4% over 20 years to invest in stocks or mutual funds, whereas that is exactly what Czech banks will do for you when you purchase investment real estate.

If you have leverage, inflation actually works to your advantage, since your debt becomes 'cheaper' with time. Thus, a 1,000,000 CZK mortgage today is not the same as what it was 10 years ago, and 10 years in the future a 1,000,000 CZK mortgage may seem like nothing.

## 2. Tax Advantages

There are a few tax advantages pertaining to property that you will not get with other investments.

For example, in Czech Republic you can depreciate your property at a fixed rate per year, which basically means you will be able to get income without paying tax on it. That's right; income without paying tax on it – how nice is that!

Depreciation is a huge advantage of property investing but can be difficult to understand. If you have trouble understanding depreciation, I would highly recommend the following YouTube videos:

Another tax advantage of property is that you can expense costs related to your property. So, for example, if you own a property in another city of Czech Republic, you can expense travel costs and hotel expenses when you visit or inspect the property.

There may be office or vehicle costs related to managing the property, and these are also allowable expenses. (Can you expense your office setup if you buy stocks or mutual funds? Not a chance. The only allowable expenses in Czech Republic for stocks or mutual funds are purchase fees and broker fees.)

In Czech Republic, a property also becomes free of any tax on the capital gains if you hold the property for five years or longer. (Whereas stocks are capital gains free in six months only if you own less than 5% of the company.)

In conclusion, property is more tax favoured compared to other investments not only while you hold it but also when you sell it.

## RUNNER-UP REASONS

In addition to the two factors above, I can add secondary reasons such as cash flow, appreciation, principal reduction and the non-volatile nature of real estate.

Real estate is also 'physical', which means you can touch and feel it, and that can be a real comfort to investors.

But before you run off and buy investment real estate, be sure to read the next chapter, which will look at some of the *disadvantages* of investing in real estate. It's not a one-way street.

*Chapter Two*

# TWO AREAS WHERE PROPERTY INVESTING CAN HARM YOU

I t would be unfair not to also talk frankly about the negative aspects of property investment.

Before you as an investor decide on property versus an alternative, you need to know how property could potentially bite you and how you can take preventative measures against potentially harmful situations.

### 1. Illiquid nature

Do you have some kind of personal situation where you need access to cash urgently? If so, don't expect to get money from your property quickly.

Illiquid means that in order to get your cash out of the investment, it usually takes months (compared to only days with a stock investment). You have to either refinance the property or sell it, both of which take considerable time.

If you need to sell it in a hurry, you may lose quite a bit of the equity that you have built up in your property. In Czech Republic, this can be due to either the bank penalties for early repayment of a mortgage or the price reduction you need to make in order to sell the property quickly.

Note that the illiquid nature of property can also be a positive thing. With illiquidity, the primary benefit is that prices move rather slowly, so it is much easier to see a market turning and act accordingly.

It can also protect us from our own emotions. Whereas a barrage of bad media headlines can make us make a rash decision regarding stocks or bonds, selling a property is a long process so it forces us to think things over.

## 2. 'Pain in the butt' factor

Under this category I include a number of points, but primarily the fact that the investment needs constant input, whether it is decision-making or additional cash. There is also a much greater time commitment to a property versus a stock or bond.

First of all, there is the time necessary to identify and get an agreement on a suitable property. It can also take days of your time to conclude all the necessary closing legalities.

If you manage the rentals yourself, you need to be able to take phone calls and give viewings when you are trying to rent the property. And you may face situations where you need to go out late in the evening to fix something in the property.

A bad tenant is a terrible situation anywhere; but in Czech Republic, where the laws are in favour of tenants, it can be a nightmare. A tenant who knows the laws can decide to stay in your flat for three or four years while you try to evict them through the courts – and not pay you rent in the meantime. If you get an aggressive or difficult tenant, it can be extremely stressful to deal with personally and cause you many sleepless nights.

Regardless of whether a tenant is bad or good, after the tenant leaves, you may need to organize painting or repairs to the apartment.

Compare this to purchasing a stock through an online brokerage and you understand why property requires much more involvement by the owner. Of course, it is possible to outsource many of these concerns to a property management company, but even with the best property management company you will have situations requiring your decision-making and input.

## ADDITIONAL POSSIBLE PAIN POINTS

To add to the two factors above, property can also cause an investor harm because it typically consumes a larger amount of the total worth of an individual than if they invested in other alternatives.

In property investing there is also the risk of liability because of injury to the tenant or damage to someone else's property, such as ice from the roof of your building falling on someone's car (a real situation that happened to a client in Prague).

## YOUR CUP OF TEA?

Phew! Did I manage to completely turn you off ever buying an investment property?

Investing in real estate is not for everyone; it requires a certain personality and a certain skill set.

*Chapter Three*

# DO YOU HAVE WHAT IT TAKES TO BE A RENTAL PROPERTY OWNER?

S elf-assessment is a very difficult thing.

Fulke Greville, an Elizabethan poet, dramatist, and statesman, is credited with saying: 'No man was ever so much deceived by another as by himself'.

Unlike other forms of investing, being a landlord requires wearing a diversified set of hats. Those who fail to make a candid self-assessment about their personal skills are often the ones who fail at property investing.

It is not the type of investment where you can sink your money into it and then forget about it.

A 100% 'do-it-yourself' landlord can be required to have a basic level of skill as an accountant, banker, attorney, bill collector, carpenter, diplomat, financial analyst, insurance agent, painter, real estate agent, psychologist, salesperson, marketer, counsellor, locksmith, social worker, plumber, etc.If you are a foreigner in Czech Republic, the above requirements can be all the more difficult if you don't have a certain level of skill with the Czech language.

As much as a successful property owner needs to have business savvy and common sense, they also need to have imperturbability. Throw in a sense of humour and you have a well-rounded investor/landlord.

A person good at self-analysis will understand that there may be some parts of the whole picture that they need to outsource, because they just know they will not be good at certain aspects of the job.

However, there are two personality traits which will prove to be a real problem for any landlord, whether he outsources some of the work or not. I call these 'guaranteed failure characteristics'.

## GUARANTEED FAILURE
## CHARACTERISTIC #1: IMPATIENT

The impatient person will find himself or herself having difficulties when it comes to negotiating, due diligence and solving problems.

If the investor is impatient to close a deal or too impatient to spend the time looking for the right property, they will purchase at a bad time or in a bad neighbourhood and/or they will pay a price above market value.

An impatient investor will not be able to stick through the ups and downs of being a landlord. As a landlord, you need to be able to be knocked completely flat and then get up, brush yourself off, chalk it up to experience, and keep going.

Bad experiences and failures are a part of any business. A successful landlord needs to be able to see the bigger picture and stick to the game plan.

Perhaps you failed to do adequate background checks on a tenant and went with your gut feeling. Now you have a non-paying tenant who you have to drag through the courts.

Or you may fail to talk to a tenant about a dog you have observed a couple of times on your property even though you have a strict 'no pet' policy in the contract. Then at move-out time, you discover that the dog has seriously damaged your wooden doors and flooring.

Experiences like these can easily convince an impatient person that property investing is not for them. They may sell their property at a bad time or not according to the terms of their fixed mortgage, which in Czech Republic can mean large penalties at the bank for early redemption.

## GUARANTEED FAILURE
## CHARACTERISTIC #2: EASILY MANIPULATED

This can be manipulation by others but also by our own emotions. This type of person will definitely have a difficult time making money as a property owner.

For example, in the purchase process, is the main criterion of an investment property the financial numbers (rent vs. price), or is it what the outside of the building looks like, the colour of paint on the walls, and the view from the window?

Right from the purchase, to financing, to finding a good tenant, to collecting rents, an owner needs to be able to draw a line in the sand and *not* be persuaded to cross it. The owner needs to have clearly in mind what is fair in each situation, not only for the tenant, the real estate agent, the property management company, and the accountant, but also for themselves as the owner and as an investor.

Are you able to keep your emotions in check and give an eviction notice when a tenant asks to pay the rent later because their pay check was reduced, they are paying for their grandmother's urgent operation, and besides, they were just mugged on the street while they were coming to meet you?

In such a situation can you explain to the tenant that you also have monthly expenses on the property, including a mortgage, association fees and ongoing repairs, all of which continue to increase in price?

## OUTSOURCING

If you find you are weak in one of the areas discussed, or, for example, you really hate crunching numbers, it doesn't mean that you should drop the idea of being a landlord. There are a number of solutions.

One solution is finding an investment partner who offsets your weaknesses.

Another alternative, which is the most commonly chosen, is to outsource those parts of the task which you are unable to do or choose not be involved in. This could mean, for example, finding a great investment advisor or property management team. In many cases, even with the additional costs, this can increase your profits because they are so much more skilled at these tasks than you are.

As mentioned at the outset, those who are highly successful at property investing are those who understand their own strengths and weaknesses and act accordingly.

*Chapter Four*

# WHO LEGALLY QUALIFIES TO PURCHASE?

T hrough the years there has probably been more confusion on this subject than any other. The confusion has been due both to the Land Registry departments themselves and to investment advisors. Evidence of this confusion can still be found by searching the topic via the internet.

### RESIDENTIAL, COMMERCIAL AND RECREATIONAL PROPERTY

Originally it was possible for non-Czech citizens to purchase residential, commercial and recreational property only via a Czech limited liability company called an SRO. (in Czech: 'společnosti s ručením omezeným').

After Czech Republic joined the EU in 2004, this changed and EU citizens could purchase directly if they had a residence permit in the country. However, this change was poorly executed by the Land Registries; the correct information was difficult to find and as a result, many EU citizens continued to purchase via an SRO into 2006 and 2007.

The change also applied to countries in so-called 'favoured nation' agreements with Czech Republic, including Norway, Switzerland, Lichtenstein and the United States. Again, there was much confusion regarding citizens of these countries, and often legal teams had to 'train' the Land Registry regarding these 'favoured nation' agreements.

The legal requirements regarding foreigners changed substantially in *May, 2009*.

From this date forward, it was legally possible for citizens of *all* foreign countries to purchase residential or recreational property directly in Czech Republic without a residence permit or citizenship. This change recognizes the EU directive (Article 56 of the EU articles of establishment) which stipulates that all EU member countries must have similar laws on the purchase of property. In fact, the directive states that there should be *no* restrictions on the purchase of property. Previously, Czech Republic had had a five-year exemption from this article, but by May 2009 this time had passed.

The directive has also proved to be true for foreign *companies*, although this interpretation of the law could be debatable, according to our legal team. In the past, foreign companies needed to establish a local branch or stand-alone SRO in order to purchase. We personally have the experience that this is no longer required and we have had clients purchase property directly with a foreign company.

Again, in many cases outside of Prague, the Land Registries may not have had experience with the purchase of property by a foreign individual or entity, so it may be necessary for your legal team to give them guidance in the current laws.

## AGRICULTURAL AND FORESTRY PROPERTY

A further two-year exemption on article 56 of the EU articles of establishment applied to the purchase of land zoned agricultural and forestry, meaning foreigners could purchase these types of land only through establishing a Czech company (SRO) or holding the appropriate licenses as a physical person.

However, this exemption expired in May 2011 under international treaties and was subsequently adopted into Czech law. So it is now possible for non-Czech citizens to purchase, without restriction, property with these zonings. In conclusion, an individual from *any nationality* can now buy *any type of property* in Czech Republic *without restriction* as a physical person.

## Chapter Five

# RESTITUTION – COULD YOUR PROPERTY BE REPOSSESSED?

R estitution is a feared word with regard to Czech property. And there is good reason for this since, given that the last 80 years has seen a few waves of expropriated property. Often it was the case that the property was expropriated from an owner who had previously acquired the property by expropriation. Let's first look at a brief overview of the history and then look at the basic restitution laws.

### OVERVIEW OF EXPROPRIATIONS

Restitution claims in Czech Republic can basically be divided into four categories.

1.  The earliest claims are connected with property which was seized from Jews when Nazi Germany occupied Czech Republic in the period from 1939 to 1945, at which time the property of Jews was expropriated and turned over to ethnic Germans.

2.   The second set of expropriations occurred at the end of WWII in 1945 under Edvard Benes, when approximately 3 million Sudeten Germans were expelled from the country and their property seized without compensation.

3.   Then when the Communists took over Czechoslovakia in 1948, there began a nationalization of private property. This was a gradual process, but it is reported that by 1989 the State owned or controlled almost all real estate in Czech Republic. For those who did receive some sort of compensation, it did not match the real value of the property.

4.   For the estimated 500,000 people who fled communist Czechoslovakia from 1948 to 1989, they also unilaterally had their property seized without compensation.

This sums up the mess of Czech real estate ownership as it came out of Communism in 1989.

## OVERVIEW OF RESTITUTIONS

Very soon after the 'Velvet Revolution' in 1989, the new government set about trying to rectify some of these past wrongs.

The easiest ones – addressed immediately – were all seizures by the Communist State from when they took power in 1948 until when they lost power in 1989. These claims were largely sorted out by 1993, and there was a 10-year limitation put on restitution claims for this period.

However, these restitutions did not address the property seized from the Jews prior to 1948 or those seized from Sudeten Germans in 1945. These have since been addressed in different decisions, which have, in general, seen compensation granted to the Jews but not to the Sudeten Germans. This is still a great source of contention.

One thing that made the restitutions very difficult to sort out was the amount of time that had passed since the expropriations. Also, in the meantime, the property had sometimes changed hands multiple times.

On January 1, 2013 there was also a decision made to return property that was formerly owned by the Churches.

At this point, in terms of being a foreign investor, it is fairly safe to say that purchase is 99% risk free from restitution unless the investor is purchasing property directly from the State. It is even more secure when purchasing individual flats rather than complete buildings. When dealing with older complete buildings, it is advisable to have your legal team research the history of ownership[*].

---

[*]  Sources for this chapter: JUDr. Daniel Burget, *The Contemporary Right to Property Restitution in the Context of Transitional Justice* by Rhodri C. Williams

*Chapter 6*

# SIX SIGNS THAT YOU ARE PERSONALLY READY TO INVEST IN PROPERTY

'Prepared for the worst but hoping for the best'. If I was going to sum up how property investors know when they are ready for a purchase, this would be it.

It is interesting that there are an increasing number of buyers who choose or plan to purchase an investment property before buying a home for themselves.

This can make good sense since for many people their personal situation can change every few years or so. What makes you choose a property when you are single can totally change when you get married, and change again when you have your first child (think proximity to work or schools, privacy, size of yard, etc.). Other life events that can make you desire a different location or type of property include changes in employment, health concerns, and the list goes on. For many this means they would prefer to rent for themselves personally and own an investment property.

Other readers of this chapter may already own a property but want to start being a landlord or add to an existing portfolio.

Whatever your personal circumstances, I recommend that you check off the following points before starting your property hunt.

### 1. Sufficient cash for the purchase

You have accumulated enough 'peníze' to cover both the deposit and the roughly 6% of property price needed for the closing costs (typical for Czech Republic).

### 2. Rent reserve

You have an emergency fund of six months of rent in case of a vacancy.

### 3. Self-analysis is positive

You are honest about what being a landlord requires and you have decided you fit the bill.

### 4. Long-term commitment

As for the deposit you are committing to the project, you don't expect to see it returned for at least seven years. Of course, it is possible to get some of it out periodically by refinancing and/or positive cash flow.

### 5. Pre-qualified lending

You have gone through the basic requirements for getting a mortgage and you comfortably fit the lender's criteria.

If you live in, or have other investments in, Czech Republic, it is very important that you are not registered in SOLUS, the national database of debtors. A registration here in most cases means either that your mortgage possibilities from major lenders will be nil or that the offered terms will be very unfavourable.

## 6. Time to devote to the purchase

An investor without a strong team already in place needs to be prepared to devote considerable time to the identification of the right property and to the purchase process. You need to be able to view the project as a second job for a given period of time.

## *Chapter Seven*

# WHEN TO STEP INTO THE PROPERTY MARKET

Timing is everything with real estate investing, but the time spans are a lot more forgiving than investing in stocks, for example.

Trying to time the bottom of a market has been likened to trying to catch a falling knife. Maybe you will get it by the handle and succeed, but maybe you will catch the blade. It's a high risk exercise.

On the other hand, if a person waits too long before buying, it can mean that the market has already changed from a buyer's market to a seller's market.

### THE PROPERTY CYCLE

For 200+ years, the property market has been closely documented and can be seen to follow a regular cycle. Of course, in Czech Republic there were major disruptions to this cycle with seizures of private property and the lack of a free market in both the Nazi and Communist regimes.

In the United States, for example, history has shown a quite regular 18-year cycle. Typically, property prices rise for 14 years and then fall for 4 years.

Search for 'real estate clock' on the internet and you will see some excellent depictions of how the cycle repeats and what the signs are for the various stages of the cycle.

Unfortunately, what we hear or read on the news can be counter-intuitive as to what the market is actually doing. So it's important to do your own research.

## WHAT TO DO NOW

The first thing you need to do is get all your ducks in a row for purchasing property. This can include making sure you qualify for a mortgage, getting your deposit together, and learning as much as you can about the property market in the area where you intend to buy.

A good thing about the property market is that once it starts to move upwards or downwards, it will not do so with the velocity of the stock market. An astute person can observe the signs of growth or decline and step in or out early. Just don't be fooled by the newspaper headlines!

*Chapter Eight*

# THINK ABOUT YOUR EXIT STRATEGY

What is your endgame? What do you want to accomplish with your investment property? How long do you plan to keep the property? These are all things that need to be considered at the outset.

A property that you purchase for retirement in 20 years could be very different from one that you purchase because you want another income stream for your household.

As well, it is very important to think about your tax strategy. This will depend a lot on where you will be a tax resident when you are getting money from the property, either in the form of net rent or capital gains at the sale.

There are basically two routes through which you can purchase property, as discussed below:

## SRO OR LIMITED LIABILITY COMPANY

### Pros

1.    Limited liability in case of a damage claim.

2.  In your place of residence, dividends may be taxed more favourably than direct rental income.

3.  The company could be used as a 'purpose of stay' for a residency visa.

## Cons

1.  More expensive setup and more expensive to operate every step of the way (from the need for a company seat, to accounting, to changes in the structure – you name it, it's more expensive).

2.  No capital gains exemption even after holding the company for many years.

3.  Banks don't want to lend to you, and when they do, the interest rates will be higher.

4.  Net profit will be taxed at the corporate tax rate, and then there will be a dividend withholding tax when you pay yourself.

5.  The bureaucracy can be a nightmare, including managing data boxes and yearly filing regulations.

## AS AN INDIVIDUAL

## Pros

1.  No capital gains tax on an investment property after five years.

2.  Net rent is taxed at the much more favourable individual rate rather than combined corporate and dividend tax rates.

3.  Much better lending terms and conditions from banks.

4.  Travel expenses from your residence abroad can be an expenditure in your accounting.

## Cons

**1.** Liability is connected with yourself as a person.

**2.** Your current tax residence might heavily tax rent and capital gains from properties which you own outside the country.

• • • • • • • • • • • • • • • • • • • • • • • • • • • • • • • • • • •

## *Section Summary*

*1. Property investment has some strong advantages in Czech Republic over other investments, including in the areas of depreciation, leverage and taxes.*

*2. A foreign national of any country can purchase any type of real estate.*

*3. You need to decide your investment goal (capital gains, cash flow, retirement home, etc.) before starting to look at properties.*

*4. Buying as an individual is much more advisable than buying through an SRO. An SRO could be better in limited situations but is much costlier to operate.*

• • • • • • • • • • • • • • • • • • • • • • • • • • • • • • • • • • •

# THE SEARCH

*Chapter Nine*

# OUR TOP TWO PROPERTY INVESTMENT RECOMMENDATIONS

A commonly asked question is what sort of investment property we would recommend in Czech Republic.

There are some properties which have proven over the years to provide the highest and most consistent returns, including through the recession that started in 2008.

Granted, investors with larger amounts of capital to invest, or who have specialized knowledge of a sector of the property market, could beat the returns of the following types of properties, but these recommendations are for smaller to medium sized investors able to invest up to 10,000,000 CZK, including funding from a bank.

The following investments are ones which have performed, and currently perform, well across most of the Czech Republic.

1. **Studio or one-bedroom apartments (1+kk to 2+kk)**

Smaller rental units have historically outperformed larger ones and continue to show higher yields.

A good strategy for investors who have enough capital is to purchase two smaller apartments (or more) rather than one large one. This has a few advantages including:

a. *Rent 'smoothing'* – You will rarely have both units vacant at the same time, meaning you are always collecting at least some rent if one unit is vacant. With one larger unit, a vacancy means a total loss of income.

b. *Ease of renting* – There are more potential renters searching for smaller flats, meaning your time between tenants will be shorter than with larger units.

c. *Liquidity* – It is much easier to sell smaller units. Also, they categorically had greater upwards pressure in the years prior to the peak and also sustained their value the best through the recession that began in 2008.

• • • • • • • • • • • • • • • • • • • • • • • • • • • • • • • • •

### *Brno small flats and pricing through 2009 recession*

*A number of UK investors bought into an apartment building in Brno on Božetěchova street (yes, the units were not chosen because of the ease of pronouncing the location).*

*The units were 23 and 35 m$^2$, and most investors bought right at the peak of the market in 2007.*

*This may seem like unfortunate timing; however, since the start of the recession in 2009 through to mid-2013 when prices in Brno started to recover, the prices have held their value, while overall Czech Republic property prices have dropped 15+%. In fact, the smaller unit is currently selling for more than the original purchase price.*

*The buyers who are purchasing the properties are either Czech investors or individuals who will use them personally.*

• • • • • • • • • • • • • • • • • • • • • • • • • • • • • • • • • • •

**d.** *Flexibility* – Your original plan might have been to buy and hold for 20 years, but an unexpected life event could cause you to need money urgently. Instead of having to liquidate a large asset, you can sell the smaller unit and keep the other one.

## 2. Multi-unit houses or townhouses ('dvougenerační' or 'vícegenerační')

Some investors have done extremely well with smaller multi-unit housing valued up to 10,000,000 CZK. The advantages of this type of purchase are:

**a.** *Complete ownership* – You do not need to pay money each month to a maintenance fund in a building where you may not see the benefits of it. There aren't other owners to deal with when making decisions about the property.

**b.** *Rent 'smoothing'* – As with smaller apartments, you have rent from multiple units instead of just one.

**c.** *Condo-izing* – It is quite straightforward in Czech Republic to divide the apartments in the Land Registry and be able to sell them as individual units. This can put an immediate premium of up to 100% on the value of your investment.

● ● ● ● ● ● ● ● ● ● ● ● ● ● ● ● ● ● ● ● ● ● ● ● ● ● ● ● ● ● ● ● ● ● ● ●

### Condo-izing – a fantastic ROI

*In 2007, my wife and I purchased a small apartment building that had four existing flats (2 x 3-bedroom units, 1 x 1-bedroom unit and 1 x studio) with the possibility of an additional one in the attic. There was also a garage in the basement. We bought it for 6,500,000 CZK.*

*The house was very out-of-date; nothing had been renovated since the 1980s or earlier.*

*First we replaced the windows and renovated all the common areas, since we knew these would provide potential buyers or renters with their first impression. This cost roughly 300,000 CZK.*

*Next we divided everything in the Land Registry so that there were 6 separate units (including the garage and the attic). At this point the flats and the garage were valued individually by a bank valuer at a total value of 12,250,000 CZK.*

*All of this was accomplished while renting the units.*

● ● ● ● ● ● ● ● ● ● ● ● ● ● ● ● ● ● ● ● ● ● ● ● ● ● ● ● ● ● ● ● ● ● ●

If you decide on a multi-unit house, be sure to look for ones which are constructed with a separate entrance for each unit, either from an outside stairwell or inside.

An undeveloped attic can be a bonus in the purchase. For a very good return on your capital, you can build a rental unit; or, if the property is divided into separate units, you can sell it to someone else to develop.

As mentioned at the outset, with specialized knowledge of a city or market sector, you may even find investments which outperform the recommended investments above. However, as a rule, we strongly believe that the above types of investments are currently the best strategy for a small to medium-sized investor in Czech Republic.

*Chapter Ten*

# WHERE TO INVEST IN CZECH REPUBLIC

L ocation is considered the key factor to a successful real estate purchase; in fact, the *three* key factors.

Not only in good times but also in bad times, location is critical. The recession and subsequent fall in property prices in Czech Republic have proven that.

Some flats have been in locations which have seen very little change in value or have been quicker to recover value lost. It has proven to be an important defensive strategy for investors to have well located properties.

With property it is so often true that you get what you pay for, and in most cases it is worth paying a bit of a premium to get an attractive location.

In this chapter we will not delve into the specific areas of each city, but rather deal with the general principals of location choice in Czech Republic.

## 1. Pick areas of population growth

Population growth in an area indicates that it is either desirable to live in and/or that there are job opportunities. Both of these are great assets for rental properties and also bode well for the long-term price growth of the property.

In Czech Republic it is possible to look at the districts and major towns and their population growth by looking at the regional stats on the website of the Czech Statistical Office.

A further breakdown into the different areas of a city is often possible to find via the city's website, but this can take some digging.

## 2. Pick an area in the city close to public transport

According to studies on public transportation use, Czech Republic leads the EU with over one-third of the population saying that public transportation is their *main means* of travel.

The Prague metro system, for example, is reported to be the seventh busiest metro system in Europe, moving over 1.5 million passengers on a typical day. This reportedly makes it the most used public transport system in the world on a per capita basis.

These statistics mean that access to public transport is a critical factor when choosing rental properties, especially when purchasing smaller properties because the tenants are less likely to own a vehicle.

## 3. Know the demographics of your potential rental market

It is also important for an investor to understand where their potential renters will be coming from. This means it is vital to have the feedback of a good local property management team that understands the rental market.

For example, in Brno over the last few years, international companies have been hiring many IT professionals. Most of their hires have been entry-level positions, and this typically means single individuals who are earning slightly above average salary.

We know from experience that these workers typically do not want to live more than a 20-minute commute away from their work. In Brno, this means you would not want to purchase a flat targeting this rental demographic in the southern part of the city because it is too far away.

As another example, in the Ostrava region there are many rentals which are targeted at workers at the Hyundai plant. Where you purchase a property targeted at Korean management will be totally different from the above example.

So it really helps to understand your potential rental demographics or to have access to a property manager or team who understands the demographics of different areas.

*Chapter Eleven*

# WHERE TO INVEST IN PRAGUE

The property market in Prague has been a favourite of property investors since the fall of communism and, with the exception of those who invested when prices were at their peak, these investors have been handsomely rewarded.

But even in the best of cities, the location, type and size of property are critical for the success of an investment. In Prague, history has shown that it is best if the property is in a traditional residential area, a district where further positive development is expected, and an area that is close to urban public transport.

Prague city is divided into 22 districts, but for investment purposes, let's focus on the most attractive of these in terms of return.

1.  **Vinohrady**, one of the most attractive Prague districts, is located in the heart of the city and has the highest density of population.

    Most of the buildings in this area are renovated to a very high standard.

Potential tenants for this location include locals and foreigners for a residence, tourists for short-term rentals, and entrepreneurs for centrally located home offices.

When choosing an apartment in this district, investors need to be very selective and patient in order to get the right price. Vinohrady can be among the most expensive areas of Prague in which to purchase. However, it is still an excellent location for investment because of the diversity and quantity of potential tenants.

2.   Locals love **Dejvice.** It is close to the centre of Prague and easily accessible by public transport.

The green Metro line 'A' will take you to the very heart of this district, and Prague international Airport is situated on the planned extension of Metro 'A'.

Dejvice is also surrounded by reasonably-priced restaurants, sports facilities, international schools and medical centres.

Potential tenants in this location are young couples, families and international entrepreneurs.

For all the above reasons, properties are easy to rent in this location and purchase prices are reasonable.

3.   **Smichov** is another one of Prague's best neighbourhoods and is a major commercial and entertainment centre.

Like Vinohrady, Smichov is highly desirable to locals and foreigners alike. People are moving to this area because, among other reasons, there is easy access to the centre and to places of employment.

An investor choosing this location would see strong rental demand and a comparatively fast appreciation in value as it continues to be highly desired.

If you look at population statistics, both Dejvice and Smichov have outstripped surrounding districts in terms of growth, demonstrating that they continue to be desirable areas for locals to live, which will continue to have a good effect on property prices.

4.   **Karlín** is a quickly developing area that has become an 'in' place to live.

Historically an industrial area, it has in recent years been revitalized with the construction of some major modern office centres. The area has also seen the introduction of many shopping and trendy dining venues.

Being close to the centre, and with the yellow metro line running right through it, the area also offers quick access to work in many parts of the city.

*Chapter Twelve*

# WHERE TO INVEST IN BRNO

B rno is second in size to Prague but could never be called second-rate.

Ask any resident why they prefer Brno to Prague and one of the first things they will invariably tell you is how much easier it is to get from one side of the city to the other and to get around in the centre.

Brno is also surrounded by a great natural environment. You can basically jump on your bicycle in any location, ride 15 minutes, and be in the forest.

Public transportation is extremely efficient and cheap in all of Czech Republic and Brno is no exception. Brno also boasts an international airport with flights to many parts of Europe . . . it is only about 130 km to Bratislava, Slovakia or Vienna, Austria.

What characterizes Brno's inhabitants? Friendly! People socialize and are friendly with others. It's part of the South Moravian open personality.

## A WELL-EDUCATED POPULOUS

Almost 25% of the population of Brno are university students studying at the Masaryk University, the University of Technology, or Mendel University of Agriculture and Forestry – just to name the largest ones.

Brno has a young, education-oriented population, which bodes well for the future and is exactly why international firms like IBM, AT&T and Monster, among others, have major centres in the city.

## RECOMMENDED DISTRICTS

Brno has **29 districts,** but I will narrow that down to the top few that we recommend for investment.

1.   In terms of districts, the majority of Brno's population lives in **Brno – centre.** However, the property prices right in the centre are very expensive compared to what you can get in rent.

2.   Prime locations in terms of investment return are **Královo Pole** and its neighbour Žabovřesky.

     These areas are close to the Technical Park (IBM, Motorola, etc.) where a lot of Czechs and foreigners are employed. Many of them are working here only on a project basis, which means they are primarily interested in renting rather than purchase. Small furnished flats (up to 50 m²) are the best rentals if you want to target this sector.

3.   Another good area for investment is **Brno – sever (north)**, specifically the districts of Černá **Pole and Lesná**. These districts have a good reputation for being the green part of Brno.

     Directly beside Lesna is the forest. This makes it an attractive location for families or couples that want to stay out of the city rush but still have an easy connection to the city centre.

     Černá Pole is also very close to the centre and offers a good quality environment for living in brick-constructed apartment buildings. These buildings are usually much smaller than the Communist-era concrete apartment buildings in terms of the number of units, but the units themselves are larger. If they are reconstructed, apartments in this area are sought after by couples and families.

4. Are there any up-and-coming districts we'd recommend?

One such area with good potential is **Brno – Zábrdovice**. This district has many old historical buildings. The negative aspect at present is that many of the buildings are owned by the municipality and are neglected. The tenants are often on social assistance and do not care for the property. However, the city is now starting to pay attention to the area, slowly reconstructing their buildings and moving out problematic tenants.

Location has always been critical to the success of investing in property in Brno and every indication is that it will continue to be so.

*Chapter Thirteen*

# WHERE TO INVEST
# IN OSTRAVA

Ostrava is the second largest city in the Czech Republic with regard to area and the third largest with regard to population.

This metropolis is the administrative centre for the Moravian-Silesian region, where over 1.2 million people live.

Ostrava is strategically located in the north-eastern part of the country, on the route of the north-south corridor between the Baltic and Adriatic Seas. Benefiting from extremely easy access to the Polish and Slovak markets, the city is the economic, business and cultural centre for the entire Euro-region.

Ostrava has excellent traffic infrastructure that includes an airport, motorways, railway corridors and an efficient integrated regional public transport system. The importance of the city steadily increases as a result of its major railway junction and the growth of the Leoš Janáček International Airport, which is suitable for all types of aircraft.

There are four universities in the city and more than 36,000 students. Instruction is provided in English by several schools, such as the 1st International School of Ostrava. The city also enjoys support from the scientific, research and innovation industries.

Major companies have chosen Ostrava as their seat, including PEGATRON Czech, Tieto, SungWoo Hitech, CTP Invest, Briggs & Stratton, ArcelorMittal, and Siemens.

With regard to the investment flow to the region, the arrival of the South Korean Hyundai Motor Company at the Nošovice Industrial Zone (near Ostrava) in 2007 proved to be a milestone, and thousands of new vacancies have been gradually created. The latest data indicates a steady trend toward a growing number of investments requiring highly qualified labour. Examples include the GE Money Centre of Customer Service and the HSBC Regional Service Centre.

## RECOMMENDED DISTRICTS

Ostrava has 23 districts in total.

1. One of the most populous districts is **Moravská Ostrava a Přívoz**, spreading out between the two rivers Odra and Ostravice.

   Besides two areas with monuments, there are many opportunities to enjoy culture and sport, as well as recreation in local parks. Because many people want to live there, the centre of Ostrava is a very good place to invest. There are opportunities to invest in new developer projects or older flats, but investors have to be selective.

2. Behind the river Ostravice, which divides the centre of Ostrava into two parts, is the **Slezka Ostrava** district. After the city centre, it is the next great area for investment, as it has new developer projects and older villas which enable people living there to travel very quickly to the centre but still live in a quiet location.

**3.** On the other side of the city is the **Poruba** district.

In this neighbourhood, facilities include the biggest summer swimming pool in central Europe, a modern ice stadium, and the Ostrava Science and Technology Park. This latter area is a top-level regional workplace, in co-operation with universities and science and research institutes, for the co-ordination of scientific and technological development in companies.

Poruba district is a very attractive area for living and definitely a good place to invest.

*Chapter Fourteen*

# WHERE TO INVEST IN PARDUBICE AND HRADEC KRÁLOVÉ

B oth of these cities are university and intellectual metropolises with 200,000 inhabitants. They boast increasingly expanding industry supported by an excellent train connection (45 min.) and motorway connection (1 hour) to Prague.

Through the <u>international airport</u> located in Pardubice, there are also good connections to countries further to the east.

Thanks to big employers such as Foxconn, Panasonic, Petrof, Synthesia-Semtex, and Kiekert, there is huge demand for rentals by foreigners.

Additionally, research that we conducted showed that there were dorm facilities for only one out of five university students; this creates additional pressure on the rental market.

### THE BEST AREAS OF PARDUBICE AND HRADEC KRÁLOVÉ

1. The best locations to invest are in **the centres** of both cities.

A major factor is the proximity to the main train station with connections to Prague.

As well, the prices of these flats in the middle of the cities are not expensive when compared to the rent achievable.

The biggest interest from possible renters in these areas is for good quality flats like 2+1 or 3+1 with kitchen appliances.

2.  The second best location for investment is **close to the Pardubice Hospital** and also the Foxconn company, where there is a big demand for smaller flats like 1+1 or 1+kk, primarily from temporary workers at Foxconn and nurses from the nearby hospital.

3.  A similar situation applies to the opposite site of Pardubice – in **Polabiny,** which is close to the biggest Pardubice industrial area, Semtin.

    In Hradec Králové, the situation is very similar; these two cities are often called twins (one is a little more weighted in universities and the other in industry).

4.  Another good location in **Hradec Králové** is around **the historic centre,** which borders part of the university and many service-based companies such as T-mobile.

*Chapter Fifteen*

# FINDING THE IDEAL PROPERTY

W e now reach the 'how' section on investment property in Czech Republic. It is great to talk about theory but all of us need help with the practical application of the theory.

One of the potentially frustrating parts of the process of purchasing an investment in Czech Republic is *identifying potential properties*. Here are a few options regarding how to proceed....

## OPTION 1: GO IT ALONE

With a command of basic Czech or a willing friend who is bilingual, it is possible to do all the leg work and research yourself.

### Pros

1.    You will get the best education and most complete picture of the market.

2.    You will find deals that you would not have found with a real estate agent.

3. You may be able to buy a property direct from an owner, meaning no real estate commission.

## Cons

1. You will have to devote a huge amount of your time to the search.

2. You will be frustrated dealing with some of the real estate agents with their typical lack of response, their unprofessionalism, and the fact that very few have exclusivity on listings.

If you decide to do it this way, the top websites for finding real estate in Czech Republic are www.bezrealitky.cz (direct from owners) and www.sreality.cz (listings from most real estate agents).

## OPTION 2: COOPERATE WITH A REAL ESTATE AGENT

As a note of caution, you should realize that there are no certifications required for real estate agents in Czech Republic. Literally, if you have roughly 1000 CZK for the trade license, you can start a real estate company.

There is also no regulation of the real estate industry. If there are any problems, you have no industry recourse and are forced to take the matter through Czech courts, or in really bad cases, handle them through the criminal system.

The purpose of this section is not to scare you but to help you realize that *utmost caution* needs to be exercised when using real estate agents.

**Pros** (with a *good agent* who understands property investing)

1. You will have the most difficult legwork done for you, which will save you a lot of frustration and wasted time.

2. You may get a property before it is advertised publically.

## Cons

1. You will only be shown properties listed by your agent, or by other agents who offer your real estate agent a good commission split.

2. You will not see any properties offered direct from owners.

3. You will still need to have your own attorney perform due diligence on the contracts.

## OPTION 3: USE A PROPERTY INVESTMENT COMPANY

There are companies, both English and Czech, that specialize in investment property, and it is possible to pay them to assist you.

### Pros

1. You will have the most difficult legwork done, which will save you a lot of frustration and wasted time.

2. You will be shown only property with investment in mind.

3. You will see properties offered directly from the owner.

4. You will have feedback on the properties that is more unbiased and objective than that of a real estate agent.

### Cons

1. You will pay more for this service than you would with a real estate company, sometimes in addition to a real estate commission.

Your choice on the above options can be determined by your personal circumstances, your command of the Czech language, your flexibility with time and your interest in property investing.

Happy hunting!

*Chapter Sixteen*

# CALCULATIONS USED TO EVALUATE PROPERTY INVESTMENT OPPORTUNITIES

To choose an investment property with your heart but not your head is not investing; it's financial suicide.

A characteristic of successful investors is the ability to remove themselves from a situation and be able to look at an opportunity objectively.

Most investors use a few calculations or gauges which they have learned to trust over time. These can be different for each investor and there are arguments for and against certain calculations.

In this chapter, I will share the ones I would typically use and why I use them.

### 1. Gross Rental Yield

This is an equation which takes the gross yearly rent and

divides it by the total purchase price of the property, expressed as a percentage.

This equation is great when you are comparing properties and you know the variables (such as loan-to-value, interest rates and expenses, etc.) will be similar. It's a quick litmus test.

## 2. CAGR over 5 years

CAGR (Compound Annual Growth Rate) is a simple way to compare the investment to other opportunities. It is better than total ROI because it is calculated according to the number of years you hold the investment.

Banks typically offer a compounding interest rate on savings. Sometimes it is compounded monthly, quarterly or yearly.

CAGR is a great way to measure stock returns since a stock can be up 40% one year and down 10% the next. By using a calculation over 5 years you can see the average yearly return accomplished.

A CAGR of roughly 15% over 5 years will double your investment. This is very achievable with a property investment. As a comparison, with a CAGR of 3% (your money in savings at a bank) it would take you about 23 years to double your money.

CAGR for a property over 5 years can be calculated by taking the yearly net cash flow (whether negative or positive) multiplied by 5, adding the amount of principal you will pay off in 5 years on the mortgage, and finally adding the expected increase in the value of the property over the same period.

To calculate the monthly mortgage payments and the amount of principal paid off over time, I use a mortgage calculator. I have come to prefer the output data on a mortgage calculator that breaks down your principal and interest payments each year.

Many property investors use the IRR (Internal Rate of Return) calculation for a property, which is essentially what I do above. However, in my personal calculations I don't include transaction costs, since all investments have transaction costs and you will likely hold the property longer than 5 years.

Many IRR calculations also include taxes. I normally don't include taxes because it can greatly complicate the equation if you start to work with depreciation and other tax deductions. It means you need your accountant involved. Suffice to say that property has a huge tax advantage over other investments.

## 3. Cash on cash

Investors looking primarily for cash flow use this metric.

It is a simple calculation of the total net cash return the investment will give (before tax) compared to the amount of cash you put in, expressed as a percentage.

The calculation is: cash-on-cash return = annual before-tax net cash flow / total cash invested.

Like the gross investment yield, this has been considered a great napkin test of whether an investment merits further consideration or not. A higher than average percentage can indicate that the property is underpriced.

A note of caution: this calculation does not take into consideration appreciation/depreciation of the asset or the amount of principal which is being paid off when a mortgage is involved.

Whenever you make calculations, it is good to work with a best case, worst case, and most likely case scenario. This helps you to see if you could financially handle, for example, mortgage interest rates going up 2%, an extended vacancy, or other variations.

## Chapter Seventeen

# CALCULATING CASH FLOW ON A POTENTIAL PROPERTY

I t is critical for a property investor to be able to work through the numbers on a potential investment property. This can greatly reduce the risk as well as help to set expectations. It is always better to be conservative in estimates.

Here are the main items in calculating cash flow on a Czech investment property and how to accurately find the value.

### 1. Incoming – Rent

The potential rent of a property can be very difficult to assess because there are so many variables and differences in property.

The best approach is to do a thorough search on websites like www.sreality.cz and www.bezrealitky.cz to find comparable properties on offer. Trying to look at properties which are similar in location, size, finish, and floor in the building is important.

Personally I also do calculations with 'best case' and 'worst case' scenarios, but in order to accurately compare different opportunities, I use a 'most likely' achievable rent.

## 2. Outgoing – Mortgage

Before getting too far, you need to understand what type of mortgage will be possible for you to get. You can speak with a bank or mortgage broker.

Again, use the most likely achievable numbers (for length of mortgage, interest rates and loan-to-value). Be sure *not* to use the numbers you see advertised on billboards or on the bank's websites without checking further. Often these are 'teasers', but they have strict criteria to get this rate and it is rarely achievable.

As well, the mortgage rates offered for a property which will be used as an investment will be higher than the rates if you were buying as a physical person. The bank views investment mortgages as a higher risk and thus increases the prices.

## 3. Outgoing – Association Fees

In Czech Republic it is typical that the tenant pays for all of the utilities which they directly consume. This includes electrical, heating, hot/cold water, and sometimes (but not always) can include cleaning of the common areas, electricity and heating in the common areas, and the expense of an elevator.

However, there are other fees which are typically borne by the owner and need to be factored into the calculation. These can be for insurance of the building as a whole as well as a maintenance fund for repairs.

The seller should be able to provide you with statements about the amounts they have been paying up until that point, unless it is a new build with no history. In fact, since January 1st, 2013, sellers are obligated to supply the

potential buyer with an energy label which rates the effi-
ciency of the apartment.

It is a good idea to also find out how much money is in
the maintenance fund. The building could be due for a
major repair such as a new roof, and if the maintenance
fund does not have enough money, each owner may be
required to cough up a significant chunk of cash. Older
buildings typically require more money in terms of ongoing maintenance so this should be factored in when
choosing a unit.

### 4. Outgoing – Vacancy

Always calculate with your property being vacant for part
of the year. A rule of thumb is 5% vacancy.

If you are managing the property yourself and you are not
very experienced, calculate with 10% until you figure out
the nuances of getting top rent and keeping your property
rented.

If you are hiring a property management company, ask
them for their track record of occupancy for the previous
years in that location.

### 5. Outgoing – Maintenance

Unless you are purchasing a new build, there will always
be small maintenance issues in the flat, and you may need
to freshen the paint between tenants or replace appliances.

The rule of thumb for maintenance on an older property
is 2 to 3% of your collected rent.

### 6. Outgoing – Property Management

If you decide you want a property management company
to take care of renting and dealing with the tenant, be sure
to get a complete picture of the costs. The more a property

management company can be geared to only getting paid when you the owner get paid (i.e. when there is a paying tenant in place), the better the chances that you will have higher occupancy and fewer defaults on payments from tenants.

In order to get a full picture of fees, be sure to ask if there are one-time fees for placing a tenant, for when the property is empty, for preparing contracts, etc.

### 7. Outgoing – Other

**a.** Property Tax

Property tax in Czech Republic is currently insignificant, but the exact amount can be obtained from the seller.

**b.** Bank Fees

Unfortunately, in Czech Republic bank fees can really add up. Many lending banks can require you to have a personal account in addition to the mortgage account.

One piece of progress in this area, though, was a court decision in Germany demonstrating that many of the additional fees charged by a bank and associated with a mortgage were illegal. After that, a class action lawsuit was started in Czech Republic against many of the banks. The majority of banks have since adjusted or eliminated the fees that are connected with mortgages.

**c.** Property Insurance

Typically you will make a monthly payment to the association of owners which includes insurance for replacement of the structure of the building, but it wouldn't replace the finishing of the apartment (i.e. kitchen, furniture, appliances).

It can be advisable to take out a content and liability insurance policy for the apartment, which can be obtained quite cheaply. It can start at around 120 CZK/month for a studio apartment, but it depends on the size and quality of the finishing, the security in the building, and whether it is in a flood zone or not.

**d.** Accounting and Tax Filing

You will need to do a yearly tax return for the property even if you don't live in Czech Republic. This can range from 5,000 CZK to 10,000 CZK per year for one property which you own as a physical person.

There are many calculators on the internet which you can use to plug in all the numbers, but sometimes they are specifically based on a certain country.

*Chapter Eighteen*

# INTERPRETING THE DIFFERENT TYPES OF PROPERTY OWNERSHIP

There are two basic forms of ownership in Czech Republic and you will see them on real estate listings as **OV (osobní vlastnictví)** and **DV (družstevní vlastnictví)**. They can be translated as private ownership and cooperative ownership respectively, and I will refer to them that way in the rest of the chapter.

Something to clear up for our readers who hail from the UK is that there is not a leasehold system in the Czech Republic. There are occasional exceptions such as with cottages where the municipality or state owns the land under the cottage, but this is a rare exception. In these cases, the cottage owner leases the property from the municipality or state on a long-term contract, usually for a very nominal amount.

Private ownership is the legal state of almost all family homes, but cooperative ownership still exists extensively in apartment blocks, although new apartment blocks are almost always in private ownership.

With **private ownership**, the name of the owner is entered directly in the Land Registry.

**Cooperative ownership** is where a legal association of the owners are entered in the Land Registry as owning the whole building. Each individual owner in the building has the 'right', much as a tenant, to use their apartment in the building.

Membership in the cooperative is governed by articles of association concluded by the members.

In many cases we have found that the articles of association stipulate that members of the association need to be Czech citizens. Often they will also prevent an SRO (Czech limited liability company) from being a member of the association.

We have been informed that legally limiting this type of ownership to Czech citizens contravenes EU laws of equal treatment, but unless the memorandum of association is changed to reflect this, there is a risk to the buyer.

However, these terms of the association need to be checked on a case-by-case basis. A non-Czech citizen does well to check this document *before* spending the time and expense on negotiating a price, starting legal work or starting a mortgage application.

Because cooperative ownership is still common, many banks offer a mortgage work-around for this type of ownership where they will give you a pre-mortgage loan. The interest rate is higher by 1 to 2% and is dependent on the ownership moving to private within a year or two. Definitely, the options are more limited, and especially so for non-Czech citizens.

Our experience and recommendation is that if you are a non-Czech citizen it is not worth spending your time looking at these types of properties.

They can be slightly cheaper than private ownership and there is a little bit of a premium that can be achieved by moving ownership from cooperative to private, but this process can be time-consuming and risky.

Moving an apartment building from cooperative to private ownership requires the cooperation and willingness of all owners, which can be a difficult thing to achieve. A single dissenting member can drag the process out and cause no end of frustrations.

We hope this helps you to sort through the OVs and DVs you see on real estate websites!

*Chapter Nineteen*

# NEGOTIATING A PROPERTY BARGAIN

N egotiation is an integral part of our everyday lives. It can be on matters as simple as agreeing with your partner where to go on holidays or with your children as to what time they need to go to bed. At a higher level it is fundamental in business dealings, salary discussions and finally, our subject – the purchase of property.

Often, much of the gain a person can get in a property purchase comes because of getting a bargain. It can give you an instant return on the transaction.

Agree to a price higher than the market and you can 'lose' your net profit from rental for two to three years while you recover this 'loss'.

The purpose of the negotiation is never to 'get one over' on the seller or other party. Unfortunately this mentality is all too common in Czech Republic.

In many cases, though, an agreement can be made for a bargain price where the seller is interested in some part of the sale process or agreement more than the actual price. It can be things like the quickness they receive their payment, whether or not the furniture or other items are part of the deal, or other issues.

Following are things which can help you to negotiate a bargain on your property purchase:

1. **Know the market** and the true value of the property.

    You should have clearly in mind the top price you will be willing to pay for the property and what price would be a great deal for you.

2. **Show respect** for the seller on all interactions.

    During the viewing, it is critical for the seller to get a good feeling about you as an individual. People draw conclusions very, very quickly and this can affect negotiations.

    Etiquette in Czech Republic includes taking off your shoes on entering a residence, greeting the seller and shaking their hand. Also, be sure to ask permission before entering rooms or opening doors in their residence.

    It can be very helpful to learn a few basic expressions in Czech in order to interact directly with the seller on a personal level. See a glossary of Czech terms at the conclusion of the book for some tips on this.

    The power of a smile can never be underestimated.

3. **Determine the reason for selling.**

    If you find out why they are selling, you can often use this to alter your offer.

    It could be that they have pressing financial needs or they need to move quickly because of a new job in another city. By meeting the needs of the seller in one area, they will often be flexible on other points, such as the price.

### 4.  Make your offer easy.

If your offer is contingent on getting financing at the bank and you haven't even talked to one yet, this will be a major negative for the seller.

By keeping the offer clean and easy it gives the seller confidence to proceed.

### 5.  Back up your offer with reasons.

Making a low-ball offer with nothing to back it up can end negotiations before you even start. If sellers have lived in the property for any period of time, they will be emotionally involved in the sale. You need to be very careful when making a low offer.

You can use comparable properties listed in the area. Or news articles which show that currently properties are selling for, as an example, 10% under the listed price. Other reasons could be uncompleted renovations, liens on the property from creditors, or a lengthy or very short handover.

Using these tips, we hope you can purchase your next property at a bargain and have the seller walking away with a smile.

*Chapter Twenty*

# DETERMINING YOUR PROPERTY PURCHASE COSTS

B efore you start, it is important to know how much the transaction costs are. This can make a significant difference in your investment calculations.

For example, in Austria, you can typically count on 9 to 12% of your property price as the transaction cost whether you are buying or selling. So if you are buying a 200,000 EUR property, you can count on 20,000 EUR in transaction costs. Transaction costs like these don't encourage 'flipping', do they?

What about in Czech Republic? Let's go through the expenses related to a purchase.

1. **Real estate fees** – 2.5% to 5% depending on which agency (plus VAT)

   The way the commission is calculated in pricing changes according to the different areas of Czech Republic. In Brno, it is additional to the price advertised and is paid by the buyer. In Prague, it is typically included in the advertised price. You don't see it but it's there!

2.   **Legal fees** – 20,000 CZK to 55,000 CZK (plus VAT)

What your total legal costs will amount to depends a lot on, first of all, which city you are buying in. In Prague and Brno, it will be difficult to find a good lawyer (especially an English-speaking one) for under 2,000 CZK/hr plus VAT.

The total number of hours will depend on how complicated the purchase is. If you include a reservation agreement, future purchase contract and purchase contract, along with liens for a mortgage, the hours really start to stack up.

You may wonder why these costs are not covered by the real estate fee, but you really cannot rely on real estate companies to protect your interests as a buyer. To proceed based on due diligence performed by a real estate company is unadvisable.

3.   **Escrow fees** – roughly 1% of purchase price

Escrows are a critical part of the purchase process and a buyer should never sidestep this in an effort to save costs.

There are some variables with this cost, depending on whether you get the escrow done at a notary office (the most expensive), a bank (middle of the road), or through a lawyer (cheapest).

Sometimes a real estate office may offer to perform this function. Even if it is free, do not agree to this. The only legal recompense to the theft of purchase money is a painful years-long process through the courts.

You can sometimes split the escrow costs with the seller, but typically the purpose of them is to protect the buyer, so often the buyer will refuse to help with this cost.

### 4. Additional fees

If you don't trust your understanding of Czech, you will need a translation of the contracts to be signed. This could run you as high as 10,000 CZK for a good, State-recognized translator and the translation of all contracts.

If you are not present to sign everything directly, there can also be an extra fee for the lawyer or someone else to represent you in signing the contracts via a power of attorney.

The fees at the Land Registry are typically split with the seller.

A rule of thumb for purchase costs in Czech Republic is 6 to 8% of the purchase price. The lower end of the range applies to expensive properties and the higher end to cheaper properties.

• • • • • • • • • • • • • • • • • • • • • • • • • • • • • • • • • •

## *Section Summary*

1. *Chose an investment property close to public transport.*

2. *Our top investment recommendations are smaller units and multi-unit houses, for both their higher yields and their easier resale.*

3. *60% of residential real estate transactions happen without real estate agents, so be willing to do some legwork yourself for the best deals.*

*4.* *Look for private (OV) ownership properties rather than cooperative (DV) ownership.*

*5.* *Purchase costs can be calculated at 6 to 8% of the purchase price.*

• • • • • • • • • • • • • • • • • • • • • • • • • • • • • • • • • • • • • • •

# THE PURCHASE

*Chapter Twenty-one*

# OBTAINING A MORTGAGE

The mortgage rules have really changed over the last 5 years, in particular with regard to non-Czech citizens who are investing in property – the focus of this chapter.

In 2006/2007 there were numerous banks vying for this type of clientele.

However, with the crisis in 2009, all banks tightened their lending criteria, particularly with regard to exactly these types of buyers. Many will not lend to non-Czech citizens at all.

• • • • • • • • • • • • • • • • • • • • • • • • • • • • • • • • • • • • •

### How CZECH POINT 101 influenced lending requirements for Hypoteční banka

*In early 2009 it became legally possible, according to the Land Registry, for non-EU residents to purchase real estate in Czech Republic without restriction.*

*However, despite the legal change, by this time all*

*the banks had tightened their lending requirements, restricting lending to the point where there was not a single bank lending to non-Czech residents without them having a residence permit.*

*At that time, CZECH POINT 101 had a very good contact at Hypoteční banka; and Pavel Pařízek, a mortgage broker with our company, showed them the internal memo from the Land Registry stating that foreigners could now purchase property without restriction.*

*This prompted them to reconsider their policies, and lo-and-behold, they no longer required residency permits as a prerequisite for a mortgage.*

• • • • • • • • • • • • • • • • • • • • • • • • • • • • • • • • •

Also, an interesting change is that while previously there were a handful of banks granting mortgages to SROs with similar conditions as those granted to individuals, this has almost totally been closed off. Currently a mortgage granted to an SRO will have much higher interest rates than a mortgage granted to a physical person; and the term offered will be shorter, typically 15 years instead of 20 or 25 years.

The general terms for obtaining a mortgage for a foreign investor are:

1.    The bank will not lend more than 90% loan-to-value. The value will be set by an internal evaluation from the bank or one of their approved contacts, and not from the purchase contract.

2.    The maximum lending period will not exceed 30 years with the most likely offer being 15 or 25 years. The length of the mortgage will be limited by the age of the borrower. Typically the mortgage will not go beyond their 65th birthday.

3. Interest rates are offered as fixed for a period of 1 to 5 years. There are a very limited number of banks offering a 'floating' rate which is pegged to the Czech National Bank rate.

4. Your personal presence will be required in a branch of their bank at some point in the mortgage process. The rest can be done via email or through a broker with power of attorney.

Generally the banks will not consider income from individual units in their equation for your eligibility for the mortgage; or if they do, they will only count a percentage of it. With multi-unit buildings this is different, and they will count more heavily the income from the building.

The *absolute best scenario* for getting a good rate and the most offers is if the foreigner: 1) lives in Czech Republic and has a long-term/permanent residence permit; and 2) is employed by a Czech company or branch which pays the salary to a Czech bank account.

Other scenarios are definitely possible, but you can expect the rate to be slightly higher and your options of banks will be more limited.

When dealing with bank reps or mortgage brokers, it is important to choose those who have experience with foreigners investing in property. A lot of time and money (obtaining documents, legal translations) can be wasted when the individual does not have experience with this particular scenario.

• • • • • • • • • • • • • • • • • • • • • • • • • • • • • • • • • •

### *Applicant refused mortgage because of being too qualified for his job*

*In a bizarre twist, there was one applicant who was refused a mortgage at a bank because he was too educated for his current position.*

*He was earning excellent money with a large, stable international company – the typical client that a bank would be eager to grant a mortgage to.*

*However, he was very well educated in a field that was different from the one he was actually working in.*

*The bank concluded that there was something strange about this applicant and no amount of persuading could get them to change their mind.*

• • • • • • • • • • • • • • • • • • • • • • • • • • • • • • • • • •

## Chapter Twenty-two

# HOW TO HANDLE EXISTING TENANTS IN A PROPERTY

I f there is an existing tenant or tenants in the property you will purchase, you need to exercise caution.

As discussed in a later chapter on landlord and tenant laws, it is very difficult to remove a non-paying tenant. Because of this, many Czech investors insist that the building be empty when they purchase it. It can even be included as part of the purchase contract with penalties associated with the seller not fulfilling this requirement.

It is definitely best if the contracts are all for a definite time. It is much easier to evict a tenant when their contract has expired than when they have a valid contract.

Although all regulated rents should now be moved to market rents, these contracts were usually made for an indefinite period of time, i.e. no ending point. What many owners have done to encourage these tenants to leave is to invest nothing into their flats in terms of reconstruction.

• • • • • • • • • • • • • • • • • • • • • • • • • • • • • • • • • • •

### *Buy-outs were common before deregulation legislation*

*In 2008 a client of ours from the US was partial owner in a block of flats in Prague. She was an absentee co-owner and asked us to advise her on matters pertaining to her property.*

*She had a tenant who enjoyed regulated rent in a 1 + 1 (studio) flat in the building. This tenant paid a mere 1 800 CZK/month when the actual market value was at least 10 000 CZK/month because of the building's fantastic location.*

*Our client had been approached by the tenant who had offeed to be bought out for 400 000 CZK so that our client could move the apartment into the free market.*

*This was a common approach to getting apartments into the free market but was quite costly for the buyer as you can see.*

• • • • • • • • • • • • • • • • • • • • • • • • • • • • • • • • • •

Another thing to be sure to have included in the purchase contract is the transfer of any damage deposits that the seller holds on behalf of the owner.

• • • • • • • • • • • • • • • • • • • • • • • • • • • • • • • • • •

### *Seller had secretly taken lump sums from tenants*

*It is sometimes the case that a landlord will take a lump sum upfront in exchange for a guarantee of low rent for an extended period of time.*

*In one building in Ostrava where clients of ours were going to purchase, Tomáš Repaský from our CZECH POINT 101 Ostrava office discovered that the seller had done this with a number of tenants, but it was not disclosed on the rental contracts. This could have been a very bad situation for the buyers.*

*In the end it was agreed that these renters would be compensated and the purchase agreements included a penalty for the seller if this was not done.*

• • • • • • • • • • • • • • • • • • • • • • • • • • • • • • • • • • •

*Chapter Twenty-three*

# PURCHASING A PROPERTY

S tarting the purchase of a property in a country other than our home one can be a terrifying experience. There is a lot of money involved – hard-earned money – so it is wise to educate ourselves on the basics of the process.

An experienced legal team will handle all the details, but it is still valuable if we understand the general steps so there are no surprises.

We strongly recommend that purchases go through an escrow account so we have included this as the default method.

There are two basics flows, depending on whether the buyer is buying with 100% cash or with a mortgage. Let's examine the steps based on these two scenarios.

Please note that there can be small variations of the methods below, but these are the basic steps.

### CASH AND FINANCED BUYER – RESERVATION AGREEMENT

Most real estate agents will push immediately for you to sign a reservation agreement, sometimes even on the first viewing.

'We have another buyer willing to pay full price tomorrow', or 'we have lots of interest in this property so we can only give you until tomorrow to make up your mind on this property' are common tactics that can be used to push you to sign a reservation agreement and pay the reservation fee.

Please note that in the Czech Republic most reservation agreements are set up in a very one-sided manner, so that if for any reason (even if it's the fault of the seller deciding not to sell) you do not complete the purchase, your deposit / reservation fee will be kept.

Based on a 2012 Czech Supreme Court decision, a real estate agent cannot keep the deposit or reservation amount as a contractual penalty.

However, in actual practice we found that the reservation agreements were a source of real contention and sometimes outright fraud. Here are some of the problems we encountered:

1. Since exclusive listings are not common, a prospective buyer would sign a reservation contract with one agency while unbeknownst to him another prospective buyer would sign with another agency.

2. The seller would not be informed or would not be in agreement with the terms of the reservation.

3. Serious negative information regarding the property would only be passed to the prospective buyer once the reservation agreement was signed and the deposit paid.

4. A very disadvantageous contract would be presented to the prospective buyer after the reservation contract was signed.

5. When the prospective buyer did withdraw for any reason, the reservation money was kept exclusively by the real estate agency and would not be shared or given to the owner.

6. Even when the seller withdrew from the agreement or substantially changed the initial terms, the real estate agency would keep the deposit.

The 2012 Supreme Court decision means that:

1.     The parties of the future agreements should be party to the reservation contract. We recommend that a buyer insist that the seller be part of the agreement.

2.     Any contractual penalty can only be demanded by the seller and not by the real estate agency. The seller may decide not to claim the penalty and the real estate agency cannot force them to do so.

Especially in a buyer's market, we encourage buyers to try to skip the reservation process and go immediately to signing of the future purchase or purchase contract.

We have found that in 99% of cases when a seller / real estate agent sees that you have a lawyer actively working on the contract, they will not offer it to anyone else.

At this point, the process divides based on whether the buyer is purchasing with 100% cash or with financing.

## FINANCED BUYER – FUTURE PURCHASE OR PRE-PURCHASE AGREEMENT

This contract is required by the banks in order to release the mortgage money. Usually it contains almost all or all of the terms of the purchase contract.

Often, at the signing of the future purchase contract and the conclusion of an escrow agreement, the deposit is sent to the escrow account. The mortgaging bank will want to see this before releasing their funds.

Also, before releasing the funds, the mortgaging bank will register their lien on the property. If it's the case that the seller already has a mortgage with a lien on the property, or by special agreement with the bank, registering the lien could happen at a later point.

## CASH AND FINANCED BUYER – PURCHASE AGREEMENT AND LAND REGISTRY

When the purchase contract has been finalized and signed by both parties, the full purchase amount is deposited in the escrow account. This can involve the complete transfer from a cash buyer or the mortgage amount sent in by the financing bank.

Once all the money is in escrow, the escrow holder submits the signed purchase contracts to the Land Registry to register the change in ownership.

All parties are notified by the Land Registry when the changes are registered. At this point the purchase price is released to the seller.

## CASH AND FINANCED BUYER – TURNOVER

The purchase contract will typically stipulate that the seller must turn the property over to the buyer within a certain number of days after receiving the purchase money from the escrow or after the changes have been registered in the Land Registry.

It is always best to have a turnover protocol signed at the time of the turnover, and to document the condition of the property and what other items may have been included (keys, furniture, etc.). Also write down all the meter numbers from the electricity, heating, gas, hot and cold water.

Typically we have found that for a cash buyer the whole process from reservation to turnover can take 1.5 to 3 months.

For a financed buyer who doesn't already have everything set up at the bank, the process typically takes 4 to 5 months.

## Chapter Twenty-four

# PROTECTING YOUR MONEY – A HORROR STORY AND 3 CAUTIONS

Through the years we have heard many buyer horror stories related to property purchases in Czech Republic. I will share one particularly shocking one with you.

• • • • • • • • • • • • • • • • • • • • • • • • • • • • • • • •

### Český Krumlov Property Purchase Horror Story

*Český Krumlov is a beautiful town in the south of Bohemia – probably one of the biggest tourist spots in Czech Republic outside of Prague and a fabulous town to visit. The old part of the town is built in the middle of a bend in the Vltava River.*

*In this beautiful setting unfolds a story that emphasizes the importance of having a team working on your side when you are involved in a real estate transaction in Czech Republic.*

*Alan and Eve Hunt from the UK had been going to Český Krumlov for about 10 years. Eve had been born in Czech Republic but had been taken to England as a very small child and she grew up there. However, regarding Czech Republic, she always said she was 'a granddaughter of the soil'.*

*As a family effort that included their children, Alan and Eve decided to purchase a house close to Český Krumlov to make their visits more pleasant and to hopefully be able to live there permanently sometime in the future.*

### The story begins in the summer of 2009 ... things start well

*In the summer of 2009, they started negotiating on a property which they had fallen in love with. The advertising real estate company assured them that they would take care of everything. A number of documents were signed and Eve was asked to wire over the purchase price of 615,000 CZK to the real estate agency's bank account.*

*This real estate agency was not a one-man shop working out of a car. Their website advertises (yes, they are still actively in business) the company as 'the biggest estate agent in Český Krumlov and one of the biggest in South Bohemia'.*

*Alan, Eve and family felt that they could trust this company and especially this agent, who was an owner of the company.*

## The horror begins

*Soon after Eve wired the money, the horror began. They noticed that the house was again listed as being for sale; and the agent stopped responding to phone calls and emails.*

*After exhausting all other means to try to contact the agent, they flew to Czech Republic in order to confront him. When they saw him on the street, he actually turned and ran away from them!*

## The police get involved

*At this point, they decided they needed to get the police involved. After hearing their story, the police informed them that this was not the first time this real estate agency, and specifically this individual, had done this, and the police wanted to prosecute him for fraud.*

*We are happy to say that the prosecution was successful; and in the fall of 2010 a guilty verdict was given and the agent was sentenced to 6 years in prison and told to repay the money.*

*However, the agent has claimed that he has no assets, so to date the money has not been returned to the Hunts.*

*To add insult to injury, the real estate agency continues to function and make money – under the direction of the culprit's son!*

## Semi-happy ending

*There is a semi-happy ending to this story in that the children were able to scrape together enough money to buy their parents a smaller cottage (with no running water) in the meantime while they try to recover the original funds.*

*To quote their daughter: 'We are heartbroken over what that so-called man did – a man with no honour or respect for people and their dreams'.*

• • • • • • • • • • • • • • • • • • • • • • • • • • • • • • • • • • •

In analyzing this story, and the countless others I have heard over the years, I would suggest that the problems and money lost could have been avoided by exercising caution regarding the following three points:

## 1. Payment of a deposit to a real estate agency

It is a worldwide practice for a buyer to pay a deposit when an agreement on price is reached with a seller.

However, the problem in Czech Republic is that the reservation (deposit) agreements which real estate agencies propose often have terms in them saying that the buyer will lose their deposit if the purchase is cancelled *for any reason.*

In one case we heard about, the buyer even had written confirmation from the seller that they had pulled out on their own volition, but the real estate agency still did not return the deposit.

Another problem is that sometimes the real estate agency that you viewed the apartment with does not even have an agreement with the seller and is not authorized to sign a reservation on their behalf.

There have been cases where even when there was a reservation agreement and a deposit was paid, the seller sold the property to another party because the real estate agent the first buyer was dealing with was not authorized to act on behalf of the owner.

What we strongly recommend is to skip the reservation contract and start working directly on the future purchase agreement. There is some associated risk that the seller may find another buyer, but this is less of a risk than trying to reclaim money from a real estate agency.

A second (but less preferred) option is to go with a reservation agreement and deposit but be sure that you have a skilled attorney check the contract. You should also confirm that the real estate agency has an agreement with the seller, and the owner should legally be party to the reservation contract.

· · · · · · · · · · · · · · · · · · · · · · · · · · · · · · · · ·

### *Things are not as they seem*

*There are many horror stories of individuals buying land only to find out it is not really theirs because the seller was not the owner.*

*In one situation, the real estate agent asserted that a number of properties for sale were owned entirely by the one seller. He strongly insisted on getting a deposit and proceeding toward the sale, but the buyer was suspicious and contacted us.*

*We investigated on behalf of the buyer and discovered that the seller was only 8/9ths owner and that the 1/9ths owner was going into bankruptcy. Of course this affected negotiations on the 'bargain' property.*

· · · · · · · · · · · · · · · · · · · · · · · · · · · · · · · · ·

## 2. Due diligence on the validity of the seller

A change in the Czech Civil Code, valid from 2014, gives credit to those who purchased property in 'good faith' based on the information in the Land Registry.

This was new because under the previous laws a seller might not have been the actual owner of a property *even if they were listed as such in the Land Registry.* Relying solely on the Land Registry constituted a high risk for the buyer.

This is because under the former Czech law, if the seller did not obtain the property themselves in a lawful way, it negated the validity of future transactions by this individual. This was even verified by a decision in the Supreme Court.

Either way, it is critical for buyers to have a legal team that can check the validity of how the seller obtained the property.

## 3. Use of an escrow account for the purchase money

In our last chapter on the Czech property purchase process, we outlined the role that escrow plays and this cannot be overemphasized. *Don't* purchase a property without the use of one.

*Never send any part of the property purchase money* to the bank account of a real estate agent or agency.

• • • • • • • • • • • • • • • • • • • • • • • • • • • • • • • • • •

### *Section Summary*

*1. Mortgages are available to foreigners under the general terms that the LTV (loan to value) does not exceed 90%, and a fixed period of 1 to 5 years is required.*

2. *Have an attorney act on your behalf rather than relying on the real estate agent's attorney.*

3. *Never pay any of the purchase money directly to an estate agent.*

4. *All money paid should go through an escrow account held by a public notary, bank or attorney. In the case of an attorney, caution is advised.*

# THE MANAGEMENT

*Chapter Twenty-Five*

# SHOULD YOU FURNISH YOUR RENTALS?

After purchasing their investment apartment, many landlords will face the question of whether to furnish it or not. There are more than a few considerations regarding this matter.

One of the most important things is for the owner to understand who their target rental market is. Sometimes this is not crystal clear at the start and takes a while to determine.

The cost of furnishing can also depend on the standard of the apartment. Furnish a luxury apartment with cheap furniture and it can actually decrease the amount of rent you can charge.

On the other hand, buying top quality furnishings for an average apartment will be a liability for you; it will not be a good investment.

When you purchase furniture for a rental apartment, you are basically entering the furniture rental business. The additional amount of rent you are able to get beyond what you would get for an unfurnished apartment *should* pay back your furniture and some extra.

Here are the pros and cons of a furnished rental:

## Pros

1.  It can (in target rental markets) help to minimize vacant periods.

2.  It reduces damages to your walls and floors since moving time can be the hardest on your property.

## Cons

1.  The damage deposit will rarely cover the cost of your furniture, meaning you can lose money if you have a destructive tenant

2.  It can become outdated in terms of style and actually turn off renters.

3.  Furniture can frequently need repairs either during rentals or between rentals.

4.  Furniture requires additional accounting, as depreciation of furniture is over 5 years whereas property is over 30 years.

5.  There is a risk of furniture theft.

6.  Some tenants may already have furniture and not want to pay for a furnished rental.

Because there are more cons than pros, we recommend that you initially offer your property as 'furnished *or* unfurnished'. You can prepare a list of furniture which you would buy if required and show this to a prospective tenant.

As a cautionary note, if a tenant agrees to rent furnished, you should have a paid reservation from the tenant before buying the furniture!

For the tenant's peace of mind, you can attach the furniture list to the reservation contract so they know what will be purchased.

Furniture should last about 5 to 7 years with normal use. However, an owner should calculate having the furniture paid back in 2 to 3 years.

In order to calculate payback, an owner needs to look at both the premium they are able to charge as well as the reduced vacancy rate (if this is the case) above an unfurnished rental.

If you do decide to rent a furnished flat, we recommend the following:

1.  Furnish at a medium to slightly above medium quality standard, and at the higher end for luxury properties

2.  Take a higher damage deposit – 1.5 to 2 months' rent

3.  Don't rent to tenants with pets, no matter their assurances to you!

Will you go into the furniture rental business? The choice is up to you.

## Chapter Twenty-six

# FINDING RESPONSIBLE TENANTS

It is one thing to find a tenant and quite another thing to find a *responsible* tenant. A responsible tenant is one that pays the rent on time and fully, and a responsible tenant doesn't damage your property.

Anyone who has owned rental properties for any length of time will confirm that 95% of the work is finding the right tenant.

This is especially vital in the Czech Republic, where the owner / tenant laws fall very much in favour of the tenant.

For example, under the current laws, in order to use a tenant's damage deposit to pay for valid damages, an owner would need either a Court decision or the tenant's agreement in writing.

### BE SURE TO HAVE OPTIONS

In many cases, owners may feel pressed to accept the first applicant because, for one reason or another, there has not been much interest in their property.

Here are our top tips for generating maximum interest in your property:

1. Get or make an accurate valuation of the potential rent.

2. Take wide-angle photos of the interior of the property on a day that has sunshine streaming in the windows.

3. Advertise your property on 'for rent by owner' websites with Czech and English text.

4. Share your property with high-performing real estate agents.

## QUALIFYING TENANTS

If you have a selection of potential tenants, you need to get down to the work of finding out which ones would make good tenants.

To do this, you need to use a combination of your personal impressions at the viewing and a thorough checking of references.

At the viewing, you can be observant about whether they arrive on time, show respect for the property (e.g. removing or offering to remove shoes) and for you (e.g. asking permission to open closed doors).

However, many owners (even very experienced landlords) have been fooled by a good first impression.

It is vital to collect *and check* references on the prospective tenant. We routinely check with their last landlord and current employer; but previous to this, we collect information about the employer and the landlord.

Giving references to a potential landlord is not common in Czech Republic, but it is a good first indicator as to whether the prospective tenant will be a cooperative tenant or not.

Our policy is simple: no references, no rental.

• • • • • • • • • • • • • • • • • • • • • • • • • • • • • • • • • • • • •

### Checking references – a national hockey hero is not excepted

*I was waiting for an arranged viewing of a flat owned by my wife and I – a rather large flat but unreconstructed. To my surprise, I saw a black Porsche Cayenne park in front of our apartment block and three big athletic guys get out.*

*My first thoughts were definitely along the lines that these guys were either: 1) Mafia; or 2) execs from a big construction company and they were looking at the flat for accommodation for their employees.*

*After I showed the flat to them, they said they were very interested and could they rent it.*

*At this point there were some communication problems when I explained to them that we needed to get references. I asked a colleague (our office is in the same building) to translate for me.*

*She explained the situation to them, and when we went back to our office to get the papers for them to fill out, she breathlessly told me that these were all famous hockey players for Brno's hockey team and that one was a national hero – Jiří Dopita. He had played in the NHL and was part of the 1998 Czech national team that won gold in the Winter Olympics.*

*After collecting the references, I asked our property manager to check them for all three renters.*

*'Phone the Brno Kometa coach'? he questioned.*

*'Yes, absolutely', I replied.*

*In my books, even a national hero is required to have reference checks.*

• • • • • • • • • • • • • • • • • • • • • • • • • • • • • • • • • • • • •

When phoning the references provided, it is good to have a crafty approach in order to weed out those tenants who pass on the name of their best drinking buddy.

Rather than stating at the start the reason for your call, tell the person that they were listed as a reference for so-and-so (provide no clue as to whether it is for rental or for a potential employer, etc.). Then ask as the first question: 'Can you please tell me how you got to know this individual?' or 'Can you please describe your relationship with this individual?' Without the initial clue that the phone call is related to rental, you can sometimes weed out the phony references.

••••••••••••••••••••••••••••••••••

### *Checking references – conspiracy foiled*

*One time I was checking references on a prospective tenant. Although she was Czech, she listed a contact and number in Germany as her last landlord.*

*When I phoned, I started the conversation with the question: 'Can you please describe your relationship with this woman?'*

*Imagine my surprise when he replied: 'She's my girlfriend'.*

••••••••••••••••••••••••••••••••••

The best question to ask a former landlord, when you are sure that you are speaking with the correct person, is whether they would rent to these tenants again if they had the opportunity.

There is no question that sourcing responsible tenants in Czech Republic takes time, but you can be assured that doing so will pay off in spades.

*Chapter 27*

# RENTAL CONTRACTS – FORMALIZING YOUR AGREEMENT

O ne of the most important factors for preserving landlord and tenant relationships is having things down *in writing*. I can cite many, many stories of relationships gone bad because of agreements not being written down. Even if both parties are well-meaning and scrupulously honest, we are, unfortunately, forgetful creatures, and this alone is reason to write everything down.

• • • • • • • • • • • • • • • • • • • • • • • • • • • • • • • • •

### *A gentleman's agreement – proof of integrity?*

*One story comes from Austria where we (myself, my wife and our three children) were to be the tenants of a new house constructed by the father of a friend of ours. Before they started building, we sat down and discussed the rental price and the general description of the house to be built. They were content to leave things at that – a general verbal agreement and away they would go spending 300,000+ EUR on a house. Sounds like the good old days of agreements on a handshake.*

*This is how things are done in Austria, I was told.*

*Well, my gut feeling and previous bad experiences told me that we needed to get some things down in writing, especially as we could have very different expectations as to who would pay for what and in what condition we would get the house. So I sat down and wrote down all the possible potential additional costs, and together with the owner we agreed who would pay for them. We also agreed what condition the house would be in when it was handed over to us.*

*In the end, we were extremely thankful that we did this, as we managed to prevent any major misunderstandings from occurring. I wish we would have included more things in the contract because we ended up getting the house with only the most basic cleaning after construction, so there were days of cleaning up before we could move in. As well, the terrace and driveway were gravel, not pavement. We had also assumed that the lights would be installed and so didn't include this in our initial agreement; but afterwards we found out we were expected to install all of them.*

*In the end, we were able to work through everything amicably, but it emphasized to me the importance of having things in writing. It's not a sign of untrustworthiness but rather the opposite – a desire to be trustworthy.*

• • • • • • • • • • • • • • • • • • • • • • • • • • • • • • • • • • • • •

## THE DIRECT RENT CONTRACT

Most owners and property managers use a normal 'direct rent contract' for documenting the relationship with the tenant.

Unfortunately the problem with this agreement is that it is controlled by the landlord-tenant laws, and these laws fall strongly in favour of the tenant. Please see chapter 28 for more information on the landlord-tenant laws in Czech Republic.

To me, it is almost suicidal for a landlord to have a tenant in place based on a direct rental contract. If you do use this, be sure to really spend the time checking the tenant's references beforehand because once they are signed in, they are in the driver's seat.

## THE SUB-RENTAL CONTRACT SYSTEM

A much better contract system to use is where the first tenant is actually *a trusted friend or close relative.* When your partner is the first tenant, there is no need to worry about the Czech landlord-tenant laws, right?

Then the tenant who actually *occupies* the property should live there based on a *sub-rental contract.* The reasons for this are as follows:

1. This relationship does not fall under the landlord-tenant laws but under a different part of the civil code.

2. The terms of the contract are directly agreeable between both parties, including the use of the damage deposit, eviction for non-payment, etc.

The only drawback to this is that you need to have two contracts. One contract is necessary for the first relationship and one for the second, so it is a bit of extra work.

Also, the rental value in the first contract should equal that of the second. Otherwise the first renter has a net profit and would need to file a tax return to claim this.

I would strongly, strongly recommend the use of this contract system for investors.

Personally, and through our company, we have used this with hundreds of tenants over the years; and it's even been taken to court so I can say that it is tried and tested.

*Chapter Twenty-eight*

# LANDLORD-TENANT LAWS FOR DIRECT RENT CONTRACTS

With the introduction of the new Civil Code in 01/2014 came a new set of laws governing the relationship between owners and tenants with a direct rent contract.

### REPAIRS

The tenant is obliged to conduct all 'minor repairs' at their own cost while they are living in the property and before handing it back to the landlord.

Minor repairs are defined as those which can be ranked under two major groups listed in government regulation No. 1095/15.

The two major groups of minor repairs which are the responsibility of the tenants are:

a)   based on the a list of items specifically mentioned in the government regulation:

- repair of any marks or damage to walls, flooring (including thresholds and baseboard) and roofs including painting

- repair of sewer and plumbing including faucets, sinks, toilets, showers and bathtubs

- repairs and maintenance of the heating / hot water system, gas or water meters

- replacement of lights, light bulbs, electrical switches, circuit breakers, door bells, home phones, internet, tv and phone connections and sockets, satellite receivers, air conditioners, central vacuum systems, alarms, detectors, etc.

- repairs and maintenance to electrical appliances in the property

- repairs of windows, doors, change of locks including electric locks for the flat entrance door, curtains and curtain rod.

**b)** based on the amount spent on the repair. In each case the repair would be less than 100 CZK/m2/year using the total area of the property and its associated parts used by the tenant (i.e. cellar space or balcony)

## RENT INCREASES

*Contracts for a limited period of time (i.e. one year)*

Unless agreed beforehand the owner cannot increase the rent unless there is a major reconstruction. At that point the amount of increase in the rent is specified in special sections of the civil code.

*Contracts without a definite length specified*

1.    The parties can either, based on § 2248, agree in the contract on the increasing of the rent, or they can do it based on § 2249, which says that in case it was not specified in the contract, the owner can propose an increase up to normal market rent in the area. The rent cannot be increased more than 20% within a 3 years period.

      § 2249 article 3 says that if the tenant agrees with the increase, they should pay the increased rent in the 3rd month after receiving the proposal. If he does not respond to the proposal within 60 days, the owner has another 90 days to submit the matter to the court.

2.    The tenant can also propose a decrease in the rent.

## CANCELLATION OF THE CONTRACT BY THE OWNER

1.    The owner can give 3 months' notice on cancellation of the contract (with or without the contract being of a definite length) based on the following reasons:

      The tenant severely violates their obligations under the lease

      The tenant is convicted of a criminal act against the owner, owner's family, other inhabitants of the property or the property itself

      It is in the public interest for the property to be vacant (for example, in the case of war)

      In case of other serious reasons ('serious reasons' is not defined so interpretation will be up to the courts)

2.    The owner can give 3 months' notice on cancellation of the contract when the contract is for an unlimited period based on the following reasons:

The owner needs the property for themselves or their relatives (marriage partner, children, brother/sister, son or daughter-in-law or their parents and siblings)

The property would be used by the owner or their partner, when they have submitted a divorce proposal and want to live separately or the couple is already divorced and one of them wants to live on the property

3. The owner can give 1 month notice on cancellation of the contract when the tenant violates their obligations in a very serious way, in particular by having an outstanding amount of three months or more of rent.

*Note: For all cancellations above, the reason for cancellation of the contract needs to be clearly stated in the cancellation document provided to the tenant.*

## CANCELLATION OF THE CONTRACT BY THE TENANT

1. The tenant can cancel a contract concluded for an unlimited time period without reason with a minimum 3 month notice period. The notice period starts from the 1st of the month following the one in which the notice was given.

2. The tenant can also cancel a contract concluded for a limited period only when their living circumstances have been changed (for example, loss or change of employment, marriage, etc.), unless something else is agreed in the contract. The minimum is a three month notice period. The notice period starts from the 1st of the month following the one in which the notice was given.

## DAMAGE DEPOSITS

1. The amount is based on agreement but should not exceed the equivalent of 6 months' rent

2. Damage deposit can be used to conduct repairs in the property (above normal wear-and-tear) and/or to settle unpaid rent

3. If the tenant does not consider the usage of the damage deposit fair they have the responsibility to challenge the owner in court

4. The tenant is due interest on their deposit at the <u>rate stipulated by the Czech National Bank</u>; however, the code only says that it should be the legal rate (it does not specify which one) so we would recommend using the "diskontní sazba ČNB"

5. Unless agreed otherwise, the owner must return the damage deposit minus any valid withholdings. The code does not specify a time period within which it needs to be returned, however it should be as soon as possible. We believe the time period a court would determine adequate would be strongly connected with the condition of the property at turn-over.

## ALTERATIONS TO THE PROPERTY

1. The tenant is allowed to paint the property and drill holes in the walls without consent of the owner (Note: the owner can require these be returned to original condition before exiting the property).

2. Based on the new civil code § 2294, if the tenant added or attached something to the wall, floor or ceiling that cannot be removed without lowering the value of the property or damaging the property, it becomes the ownership of the owner. As well, if the tenant did not ask the owner for the permission to do it / nor was given permission, the owner is not obligated to pay the tenant for these alterations.

## PETS

Owners cannot restrict tenants from having pets in the property.

## SUB-RENTING

A tenant can sub-rent the property to whoever he wants. As long as they stay in the property, they do not need consent from the owner. The owner has the option to limit the amount of people who would be allowed to live in the property based on normal usage (i.e. studio maximum of 2 people, 2+kk or 1 bedroom maximum of 4 people).

*Recommendation to owners: Put the maximum number of people allowed to live in the property in the contract to prevent abuse of the sub-rental law.*

## RESALE

If an owner with a multiple unit building divides the building into individual units for resale, they must first offer it to the tenant at the asking price. The tenants have 6 months to decide if they will buy it.

## ENTERING THE PROPERTY – REPAIRS, VIEWINGS AND INSPECTIONS

1.  With the exception of an emergency (flood, fire, etc.), the owner is not permitted to enter a property without consent of the tenant. The following are reasons the owner can give written notice for permission to access his property:

    • repair or maintenance of critical systems such as heating and water

    • repair or replacement of equipment which is included in the rented property

    • reading and recording meter numbers associated with heating, gas and water.

2.  Access has to be agreed in the contract otherwise the owner is not allowed to access the property for other reasons without permission from the tenant.

3.  If the tenant is leaving for more than 2 months they need to inform the owner who will be their representative to open the property. If he doesn't let the owner know the owner automatically becomes the representative and can access the property. It also gives the owner the right to cancel the contract with a 3-month notice period.

    *Recommendation to owners: terms of a visit can be agreed in the contract, for example, 48 hours' written notice is given and then the tenant explicitly agrees that the owner can access.*

## UTILITIES

Calculation of utility payments needs to be based on code 67/2013.

## ADDITIONAL OCCUPANTS

When there is a variation in the number of tenants from the original contract, the tenant is obliged to inform the owner of this change within 2 months. As per the section on sub-renting, the owner can also limit the number of tenants living in the property to what would be normal based on the size and equipment of the property.

## CHANGING OF LOCKS

1.  An owner cannot change the locks on a property in case of non-payment of rent.

2.  The tenant can change the lock and there is no obligation to inform the owner or provide them with a key

## USING THE PROPERTY FOR BUSINESS

The tenant can run a business out of the property without the owner's explicit consent if the nature of the business wouldn't damage the property.

## PAYMENT OF RENT

The tenant can pay the rent up to the 5th day in a month for the month of rent, unless a later date has been agreed (earlier dates can be agreed but tenant can pay up to the 5th without any penalty).

*As the landlord tenant laws in Czech Republic changed relatively recently, many matters will still need to be decided in court before we can have an exact interpretation of the laws.*

# Chapter Twenty-nine

# TOP POINTERS FOR RECEIVING TIMELY RENT PAYMENTS

Collecting rent from your tenants in a timely fashion is critical to your property being a 'passive' investment. Otherwise, you can spend hours every month dealing with money transfers and chasing your rent payment.

As we stated in a previous chapter on how to find the best tenants, 95% of the work is in the selection process.

However, even with good tenants there can be a need to do some training – training so that the priority of your rent payment goes from below vacations and new clothing to being right at the top along with food.

How can a landlord accomplish this?

One important thing is to remind the tenant that you also have monthly obligations you have to meet. Sometimes a tenant may have the idea that the landlord is just sitting back, semi-retired. If you have a monthly mortgage payment, tell them that you need their rent to pay this; and tell them there are additional building fees you have to pay such as insurance or common area costs.

| PRIORITY | DESCRIPTION | PRIORITY | DESCRIPTION |
|:---:|:---|:---:|:---|
| 1 | Food | 1 | Food |
| 2 | New iPhone | 2 | Rent |
| 3 | Mountain biking excursions | 3 | Mountain biking excursions |
| 4 | Winter vacation to Spain | 4 | Winter vacation to Spain |
| 5 | New tires for car | 5 | New tires for car |
| 6 | Gift for second cousin's new baby | 6 | Gift for second cousin's new baby |
| 7 | Rent | 7 | New iPhone |

*Where you need the rent payment in your tenant's priority list*

There are also 'push' and 'pull' techniques. Here we'll discuss both of them and what we have found to work best.

## 'PUSH' TECHNIQUES

Push techniques are those which motivate the tenant on the basis of negative consequences.

This can be fines or penalties for late payment.

We would recommend including in the rental contract a specific percentage penalty for each day of late payment.

## 'PULL' TECHNIQUES

Pull techniques are those that reward a tenant for paying on time.

For example, the contract could be structured so that if the tenant pays by a certain date, the rent is 'discounted' to 10,000 CZK, but after that the price goes up by 100 CZK/day. It is sort of the same as a penalty but is a little more appealing to the tenant. Everyone loves a discount.

One pull technique that we have used with good effect is that if a tenant pays their rent on time every month for 12 months and renews their contract for a year, they will get a half month of free rent at the start of their second contract.

A further pull technique we have used to good effect for the last 4 years is to enter all tenants who have paid their rent on time for the previous three months into a draw. Two or three tenants are drawn as the winners of prizes such as digital picture frames, gift vouchers at restaurants, etc. The tenants are delighted and it creates good word-of-mouth about your rental properties. Of course, for this to work you need to have a number of tenants.

## WHAT'S WORKED BEST

We have found that a combination of push and pull techniques works best.

Our contracts have both the 0.5% penalty for late payment as well as a bonus at renewal when they've made 12 months of timely payments.

And, we still use the tenant draws. That's fun for us too!

Hopefully some of these suggestions will be useful to you and you can achieve timely rent payments from your tenants.

Please write me if you have questions about these tactics or if you have found additional ways that work for getting tenants to pay their rent on time.

*Chapter Thirty*

# RETAINING RESPONSIBLE TENANTS

Congratulations! You've managed to source a responsible tenant – not an easy feat. It is great to have your rent paid on time each month, and from your visits to your property, you can also see that it is being taken care of.

However, on the other hand, a responsible tenant often knows their own value and if you take them for granted you could lose them. They are, after all, your customers. Every business owner knows that if they don't appreciate their customers, their business will fail.

Here are a few things you can do to show your tenant that you value them as an individual and as a renter, and ultimately you will keep them longer as your customer.

### 1. Get to know their names.

There's nothing that demonstrates more that you don't matter to someone than not remembering their name after numerous meetings.

If you can also remember family member names, or additional details such as where they work or a recent vacation, this is a bonus and will show them that you are interested in them as an individual.

A word of warning, though, about Czech tenants: they can view additional questions as intrusive rather than a display of personal interest, so tread carefully.

## 2. Show good listening skills when your tenant speaks.

Perhaps it seems like a no-brainer, but keeping your mouth shut and ears open, maintaining good eye contact, and asking appropriate questions shows personal interest. Just because you own a rental property does not make you superior to your renter in some way.

## 3. Don't enter the property without proper notice and elicited cooperation.

It's true that you own the property; but while the tenant is there, it could be viewed as break-and-enter to go into it without appropriate notice.

Even if a tenant doesn't call the police on you, the fact that you didn't respect them as the current resident can be very irritating for them.

## 4. Redecorate before, rather than after, a tenant leaves.

Owners typically redecorate between tenants. However, if your property is getting outdated or in need of freshening up, and a good tenant has been there for two or three years, you can be sure that the tenant also notices this eventuality. If you freshen the apartment up while they're still living in it, it may prevent the tenant from giving notice.

By doing a few basic things like these, you can show your responsible tenant that you appreciate their business and want to keep doing business with them into the future.

*Chapter Thirty-one*

# RESOLVING TENANT PROBLEMS

E very relationship can have difficult moments, and this is also true in the owner and tenant relationship. And some-times the problems can get out of hand if not handled properly, as I have personally experienced.

• • • • • • • • • • • • • • • • • • • • • • • • • • • • • • • • • • •

### *A tenant dispute gone bad – death threats*

*Early in my property managing days in Brno, a damage deposit disagreement between a tenant and myself got rather personal, resulting in me receiving death threats from the tenant. He even came by our apartment one evening, and when we didn't answer the door he scratched a huge X with his keys on our door.*

*Needless to say, this caused no little amount*
*of stress for myself and my wife as we had a*
*newborn in the apartment.*

*We immediately called the police, who were*
*extremely supportive, and one of the officers even*
*gave us his personal mobile number so we could*
*phone him at any time if the tenant showed up*
*again.*

*The disagreement was over a measly 4000 CZK.*
*The reason I stood my ground was because it was*
*a client's flat, but in retrospect it would have been*
*better for me to cough up the deposit out of my*
*own pocket rather than go through the stress that*
*it put our family under.*

• • • • • • • • • • • • • • • • • • • • • • • • • • • • • • • • • • • •

How can a landlord go about resolving tenant problems, whether it be the responsibility of a repair, a rent increase, or the use of the damage deposit (the most common friction point)?

Both tenants and landlords can avoid a disagreement escalating to legal action or worse by taking the following steps.

### 1. Make sure potential points of conflict are addressed in your contract.

Prevention is the best way to avoid problems.

The contract should clearly address common areas of disagreements including repairs and damage to the apartment.

It is best to ensure that all communication on these matters is done in writing. Otherwise, it's a 'he said / she said' scenario.

For example, if there are major defects in the property (say a leaking pipe), it should be in the contract that the tenant needs to notify the owner in writing without delay; otherwise resulting damages could be their responsibility.

It is also critical to have a thorough turnover document which documents the state of the apartment at the time of rental and which can be used to compare the condition at the move-out. A digital camera is perfect for having visible proof which is hard to dispute.

The landlord needs to also keep records of any phone conversations, and it's best to confirm the conversation in an email to the tenant, so you have things in writing.

## 2. When discussing potentially explosive topics, use the personal touch.

In our age of digital communication, it is easy to fire off an email to deal with a situation.

However, the order of preference when dealing with potentially explosive situations is: 1) they are best done in person; 2) second best is via a phone call; and 3) the last option should be email.

The reason for this is that emails can be read in very different ways by different people. If the topic is already potentially divisive, the receiver can read things into the tone of the email that were not intended.

I'm not saying that you shouldn't confirm things by email; but it's best to first discuss in person or over the phone and then confirm via email.

## 3. Know your rights and obligations under the law

It is good to know where a person stands according to the law.

In the case of a normal direct rent contract, the landlord needs to be aware that in some aspects the law is very much in favour of the tenant.

In the case that the tenant is living in the flat via a sub-rental contract, the terms of the contract can be agreed by both parties.

*Note of caution:* In a tenant dispute, it is rarely a good tactic to immediately start quoting the law because this can quickly escalate it into an actual legal dispute. It is best to start on a personal level and try to resolve the dispute through dialogue.

• • • • • • • • • • • • • • • • • • • • • • • • • • • • • • • • • •

### *Eviction of a non-paying tenant in Zlín – with police backup*

*With a sub-rental contract system, it is possible to agree to the terms of eviction.*

*In the case of non-payment, it is possible to send the tenant a cancellation of the contract, giving the tenant a certain amount of time to move out of the property.*

*If they refuse, our policy is that we post a note on their door saying that they should move everything out by such-and-such a date as the locks will then be changed.*

*In Zlín we had a non-paying tenant who refused to move out after legal notice and a notice posted on her door. Two members of our property management team went to the apartment to move her things into a storage room. She was not home at the time so they changed the locks and started the moving process.*

*After the moving was about 75% complete, the tenant came home. When she began to physically prevent our property management team from removing our items, they phoned the police. When the police arrived, they took down both sides of the story. Our property managers had the contracts and all supporting documentation.*

*After discussing the matter together, the police informed the tenant that we were in the right and that she needed to move all her things out of the building immediately.*

*This was a sub-rental. Try this with a direct rent contract and the police will back the tenant up unless you have a court order!*

• • • • • • • • • • • • • • • • • • • • • • • • • • • • • • • • • • •

### 4. Use a third party to mediate

In some cases when it is not possible to resolve the issue directly with the tenant, it is good to involve a third party to mediate between the two parties.

This is because these problems often become a personal issue between the tenant and the landlord. By having a third person in the middle, the personal element can be defused and both parties can think more rationally.

Hopefully, by paying attention to the above suggestions, any legal action can be avoided and matters solved fairly for both parties.

*Chapter Thirty-two*

# ASSOCIATION OF OWNERS FEES – WHO PAYS WHAT?

A ssociation of owners fees are the reality of every apartment or flat owner. In other countries the legal entity that the owners form can be called a condo, commonhold or homeowners association. In Czech Republic it is called a 'společenství vlastníků jednotek' or SVJ for short. We will call it an association of owners for the remainder of this chapter.

Many owners who are renting their property leave thousands of CZK on the table because they have problems with the association of owners' statements. Either they don't understand the statements they receive and/or they don't know which items the tenant should be paying.

In many cases, tenants can be asked to cover the entire bill. However, often the rent must then be reduced. Most tenants are looking at the total cost rather than only the rent.

# ASSOCIATION OF OWNERS STATEMENT – UNDERSTANDING THE CHARGES

Below is a typical statement you would receive from an association of owners. We will step through its parts (they are numbered in the example below) and explain the meaning of each. Also we will identify whether it is normally paid by the tenant or the owner.

```
│ Dne: 17.05.2015                         DES Domovní Evidenční Systém
            EVIDENČNÍ LIST
        pro výpočet úhrady za užívání bytu

 ┌──────────────────────────────┬──────────────────────────────────┐
 │ Správce                      │ Vlastník nemovitosti             │
 │ Spravce super .s r.o.        │ John Doe                         │
 │ Videnska 51a                 │ Vodní 14 1001                    │
 │ Brno                         │ 60200  BRNO                      │
 │ 602 00                       │ IČ:        č.ú:                  │
 ├──────────────────────────────┴──────────────────────────────────┤
 │ Uživatel : DOE JOHN                                              │
 ├──────────────────────────────────────────────────────────────────┤
 │ Adresa   : Vodni 14 0/1001.00            Číslo bytu :     26.0   │
 │ Obec-část: BRNO            PSČ : 60200   Variab.symb.100100026   │
 ├──────────────────────────────────────────────────────────────────┤
 │ Kategorie 1  Kuchyně N  Počet obytných místn.  3 │Počet osob evidenční 2│
 │ Příslušen.:  ZÁKLADNÍ                             │ #1     pro služby  2 │
 │ Podlaží   2  Napětí 220 STA   0 Komíny 0 Výtah A │                      │
 │ Topení    :  ÚSTŘEDNÍ                             │ Přidělen od 01.03.2015│
 │ Vodné     :  0056-VÝTOK WC, KOUPELNA CENTRÁLNÍ P │ Nájem na dobu neurčitou│
 └──────────────────────────────────────────────────────────────────┘
```

| | Výměr úhrad za užívání bytu ( služeb ) | | | | | | | |
|---|---|---|---|---|---|---|---|---|
| #2 | Vodné-stočné | 260 | Teplo | #9 | 1528 | Ohřev TUV | #15 | 0 |
| #3 | Uklid | 202 | Odpadky | #10 | 0 | Výtah | #16 | 65 |
| #4 | Kominy | 0 | Spol.el. | #11 | 50 | STA | #17 | 0 |
| #5 | Prádelna | 0 | Stočné | #12 | 0 | Splašky | #18 | 0 |
| #6 | Fond oprav | 512 | Daň z nemov. | #13 | 0 | Pojištěni | #19 | 50 |
| #7 | Správ.popl. | 155 | Hypotéka | #14 | 0 | Ostatní slu | #20 | 17 |
| #8 | Ostatni slu | 150 | | | | | | |

```
 ┌──────────────────────────────────────────────────────────────────┐
 │ Platba: Složenkou      Od 05/2015  Celkem předepsáno  2989.00 Kč │
 └──────────────────────────────────────────────────────────────────┘

 Rozpis mistností
```

| Mistnost | Celkové m2 | Započt. plocha teplo m2 | Způsob vytápěni | Podílové m2 |
|---|---|---|---|---|
| | 102.40 | 102.40 | ústřední | 102.40 |
| terasa | 25.40 | #21 0.00 | žádné topeni | 0.00 |
| | 127.80 | 102.40 | | 102.40 |

An owner needs to be aware that the association of owners statement and its fees that you receive *are an estimate* based on actual costs from the previous year. The association of owners will usually read the meters and make all calculations *for the previous year* for actual usage in the spring.

1.  **Počet osob evidenční | Number of people living in the apartment** – This is critical to keep accurate as many calculations are based on the number of occupants. If your flat is empty for longer than a couple of weeks be sure to notify the SVJ.

2.  **Vodné-stočné | Cold water** – Paid by: tenant

3.  **Úklid | Common area cleaning** – Paid by: owner

4.  **Komíny | Chimney** – Paid by: owner

5.  **Prádelna | Common laundry area** – Paid by: tenant

6.  **Fond oprav | Maintenance fund** – Paid by: owner (This is a fund for repairs of the common areas of the house.)

7.  **Správ.popl. | Building management fee** – Paid by: owner

8.  **Ostatní slu | Other services** – Paid by: owner or tenant depending on what is included

9.  **Teplo | Heating** – Paid by: tenant (when your heating comes from a common source in the building and the costs are shared)

10. **Odpadky | Garbage** – Paid by: tenant

11. **Spol.el. | Common area electrical** – Paid by: owner

12. **Stočné | Water distribution costs** – Paid by: tenant

13. **Daň z nemov. | Property tax** – Paid by: owner

14. **Hypotéka | Mortgage** – Paid by: owner (this can be here if the SVJ takes a mortgage to pay for maintenance or repair work)

15. **Ohřev TUV | Hot water** – Paid by: tenant

16. **Výtah | Elevator** – Paid by: tenant

17. **STA | TV Antennae** – Paid by: tenant

18. **Splašky | Sewage** – Paid by: tenant

19. **Pojištění | Insurance** – Paid by: owner

20. **Ostatní slu | Other services** – Paid by: owner or tenant depending on what is included. This can include, for example, payment of the person who represents the association of owners, in Czech called the 'předseda'.

21. **Započt. plocha teplo m2 | Size of the heated area of the flat** – This is very important to be accurate as while some calculations are based on the number of occupants, others are based on the size of your flat.

## ASSOCIATION OF OWNERS FEES – OUR RECOMMENDATION

What we do, and what we recommend a rental owner does, is to *collect 25% to 50% more than the deposit amount monthly*. This is because:

- The actual association of owner costs usually go up during the year while you are still paying last year's deposits

- The tenant may consume much more heating/electricity/water than the previous occupant

- It is extremely hard to collect additional costs after the tenant has vacated the apartment, which may have happened by the time you get your statement from the association of owners for the previous year.

Please remember that when the tenant requests a reconciliation of the time they lived in the apartment, the owner is required to do this. This means they should keep very accurate records of the meter readings before and after the tenant leaves.

*Chapter Thirty-three*

# FOUR TIPS FOR BOOSTING YIELDS

P ositive or neutral cash flow should always be a main concern for the property investor. Without this, your investment days are limited.

A surprising amount of water can result when an eaves trough collects small drops from a large surface.

In the same way, every small tweak you can make to your property's cash flow can compound over the years to add up to a sizable sum.

Below are our top tips for boosting the rental yield you can get from a Czech rental property.

1. **Minimize or eliminate bank fees** (savings: 200 to 500 CZK per month).

   Bank fees in Czech Republic can border on the ridiculous, and they can be particularly harsh for SROs.

   A typical owner of a property via an SRO with a mortgage can have an SRO bank account, an account connected to the mortgage, and the mortgage account itself. Each can have administration fees adding up to thousands of CZK per year.

For SROs, as with individuals, there are now banks, such as Fio banka, which offer bank accounts with no monthly or transaction fees.

**2. Make sure your property is not insured twice** (savings: 100 to 500 CZK per month)**.**

Often, investors have purchased a separate property insurance policy without realizing that their monthly contribution to the association of owners includes an amount for property insurance. The association of owners' policy is taken out on the whole building and would include replacing their individual flat.

You will never get paid out twice for an insurance claim, so you may be able to drop the individual policy.

**3. Collect water usage and common area fees from the tenant** (savings: 250 to 500 CZK per month)**.**

In Czech Republic it is common for the tenant to pay not only for electricity and heating but also for water usage, elevator maintenance, cleaning of the common areas and garbage collection.

**4 Transfer utilities to the tenant or collect more than the suggested deposit** (savings: 200 CZK + per month)**.**

We have found the absolute best strategy is for any utilities with a separate meter to be transferred to the name of the tenant.

The reasons for this are: 1) They are directly responsible to the company for their usage; and 2) Collection of underpayment becomes the responsibility of the utility company and not you as the owner.

In the case that it is not possible to transfer the contracts, we recommend collecting 15 to 25% more each month than the utility company's monthly deposits. The reason for this is that normally the meters are read only once per year. The actual consumption of a tenant can be much higher than their monthly deposits (this year's deposits based on the previous year's usage). Too often we have seen an owner stuck with a large utility bill and the tenant gone.

*Chapter Thirty-four*

# SIX TIPS TO ACHIEVE MAXIMUM OCCUPANCY

There is nothing worse than an 'investment' that you have to continually pour money into. Sometimes a rental property can seem more like a sieve than a bucket in which to build your assets.

One of the holes that might be leaking water with your rental property is your occupancy. Here are some tips to plug that hole and keep more of the water in your bucket.

First of all, let's define occupancy.

It is the percentage of the year that you have a paying tenant in your flat. Thus a 95% occupancy rate means that there are only 2 weeks in a year when you don't have a paying tenant.

1. **The optimal occupancy range is between 93 and 97%.**

   Occupancy of less than 93% means that you are bleeding money by having your flat empty too much of the year.

   Occupancy of more than 97% ongoing means that you are probably not charging enough for rent, which means you are also losing money.

## 2. Get bright, wide-angle photos and preferably a video for advertising.

Spend the time if you can do it yourself, or pay someone to take professional, wide-angle photos of your property on a day the sun is streaming in through the windows.

It is amazing how much of a difference exceptional photos make when it comes to the number of inquiries. If you do this at the start, you can use the same photos for years as long as the fundamentals of the flat do not change.

## 3. Give yourself enough lead time.

You should be contacting your tenant three months before their contract is due to expire, asking them whether they will be renewing or not.

It is also necessary to set a deadline by which the renewal needs to be signed. Typically it is best to say two months before the contract expires. This gives them a month to decide what they will do, which is ample time for most tenants.

If the tenant informs you that they will not be renewing, this gives you 1.5 to 2 months of lead time to begin advertising for a new renter.

## 4. Pre-qualify tenants.

You might wonder how pre-qualifying tenants improves your occupancy; isn't the most important thing just to get them in?

Well, if you have a tenant but they don't pay rent, it is the same as your flat being empty. In fact, it is often better for your flat to be empty.

The amount of time and emotional energy that it takes to deal with a non-paying tenant is amazing. Invest a little at the start to weed out the bad ones.

## 5. Collect a substantial damage deposit.

There is a fine line between asking for too big a damage deposit which would eliminate potential tenants and having enough to protect your interests.

We have found the 'sweet spot' to be 1.5 times the monthly rent and utilities.

How does this affect your occupancy?

A major factor is that it discourages tenants from moving out without notice. As well, if they do move out without notice, you have enough damage deposit to carry you through to the next tenant, meaning no vacancy.

Currently the maximum allowable damage deposit that can be collected is 3 months rent, and under the new civil code (in 2014) it will be 6 months.

Of course, in order to use the damage deposit to cover rents, you need to get either a court order or the tenant's approval, or use the contract system in Tip 6 (below).

## 6. Have a contract system that allows evictions.

Don't get me started talking about the landlord-tenant laws that fall strongly in favour of the tenant. I could rant on for hours.

A much better solution is to use a sub-rental contract system whereby the tenant who actually is in the property is there on the basis of a sub-rental contract. This contract falls outside of the landlord-tenant laws and basically whatever you agree with the tenant is what is applicable.

This allows you to quickly evict a non-paying tenant rather than waiting possibly years for the court to evict them.

Hopefully the above information will help you plug any holes that may be turning your bucket into a sieve.

*Chapter Thirty-five*

# RENEGOTIATING OR REFINANCING YOUR MORTGAGE

Achieving a good mortgage interest rate can make the difference between a cash flow negative property and one which is paying you out monthly.

The time spent on this can pay off in a big way.

● ● ● ● ● ● ● ● ● ● ● ● ● ● ● ● ● ● ● ● ● ● ● ● ● ● ● ● ● ● ● ● ● ● ● ● ●

### *Our refinancing story –*
### *how I earned 45,000 CZK per hour*

*In 2007 my wife and I, together with family, bought a rental house in Brno with four flats in it and the potential for a fifth to go in the attic. We got a 90% LTV mortgage for a total of 5,500,000 CZK. With a 3.5% interest rate over 30 years, the initial cash flow was fantastic. Our gross rent was close to 40,000 CZK and our mortgage payments 25,800 CZK. It had a 7.3% gross rental yield with potential for additional increases in value by developing the attic space and dividing the building into separate living units to be sold individually.*

*We fixed the mortgage for only one year because we planned to divide the flats into separate living units (in Canada we call this 'condo-izing'), and this would cause a change to the mortgage agreement. Changes made to a mortgage agreement at the time of fixation don't carry the high penalties of those done outside fixation.*

*What a shock we received in year two when the interest rate jumped to 5.58%, increasing our mortgage payments to 31,500 CZK.*

*In the subsequent years, we managed to get the flats legally divided and re-evaluated and then the liens lifted off all of the flats except for two. This lowered the actual LTV based on the new valuations to 71%.*

*You would think this would mean a greatly reduced risk assessment by the bank and subsequently better mortgage rates. Well, think again.*

*Even with the base mortgage rate moving lower, the banks in Czech Republic continue to keep their lending rates at the same level or at a higher level than before. Especially with foreigners, and for anyone who was getting or had mortgages for investment properties, they kept the rates very high.*

## Our Czech bank's mortgage offer – 2011

*This spring, with the news everywhere that mortgage rates were heading down, I waited eagerly for our yearly mortgage renewal offer, hoping for a much better rate.*

*Imagine my disgust when our offer came in at 5.5% for a one-year fixed mortgage and 6.09% for a five-year fixed mortgage. Only slightly lower than the year before. I was choked!*

*If there is one thing I can't stand and am very vocal about, it is the blatant greed of the major Czech banks, and in my mind, this was just another example.*

*At this point came one hour of my four hours spent on this renegotiation as I ranted to my wife about the greed of Czech banks. She is somehow an expert on the subject, even though I manage all our banking.*

*The good thing is that our company has a mortgage advisor in-house who is experienced in handling mortgages for foreigners. I immediately spoke with him to get an idea of whether we could move our mortgage elsewhere.*

*Unfortunately for us and many other foreigners, there was a strong barrier to changing mortgage providers because:*

1. *There were not many mortgage providers who would lend to foreign investors.*

2. *Any provider who did lend required personal presence at least one time in the process – really a pain for us with our co-investors living in Canada.*

**3.** *The longest mortgage offered for an investment property was 20 years, compared to the 30 years previously possible. This would really have squeezed our cash flow.*

### Renegotiating our mortgage

*After determining that the mortgage offer we had received was very high – in fact, extremely high – based on the LTV and our good repayment history; I set about trying to renegotiate the mortgage or change mortgage providers.*

*First, our mortgage broker sent out our basic finance details to those banks who would possibly give us a mortgage to see what offers we would receive.*

*Second, I wrote a polite but very strong email to our current Czech mortgage bank stating the reasons we considered the offer poor, why we were good clients for them (LTV was now low and we were always on time with our payments), and that we were in the process of getting offers from other banks. In my email, I plainly stated that we thought a mortgage offer 1% less would be in line with other current offers.*

*Imagine my surprise when I received a phone call the next day from someone at the bank saying that they could offer me a reduction of .8%. After a few more days of negotiations, we settled at a 1% discount for the 5-year fixed.*

*The 1% difference worked out to 3,000 CZK a month of interest we will save by not having accepted their first offer. Over a 5-year period this saves us 180,000 CZK.*

*I estimate I spent a total of four hours on the renegotiation, including the one hour ranting to my wife after receiving the first offer, then one hour spent with our mortgage broker talking about alternatives, and finally two hours negotiating with our current bank.*

*This works out to a payment of 45,000 CZK per hour. Not too shabby.*

*Before and after this personal experience, we have also assisted our clients with many, many renegotiations.*

• • • • • • • • • • • • • • • • • • • • • • • • • • • • • • • •

Here are the top lessons we have learned.

### 1. Make sure you keep your mortgage up-to-date and not in default.

It is important to be aware that all the major banks (and most telecoms plus others) in the Czech Republic share data regarding debtors through SOLUS, a national registry of debtors.

There are other registers as well which different banks contribute to and check when performing background checks on an applicant.

Unfortunately, banks don't seem to currently differentiate between petty debt default and substantial debt default. Most have a zero tolerance policy. We have seen individuals with a default of a couple thousand CZK to a telecom company being blocked from getting a mortgage. As well, you will be unable to negotiate with the lender who currently holds your mortgage for a better rate because they will judge you as high risk.

If you did have a period of default, you should at least try to keep your mortgage up-to-date for as long as possible before your fixation comes up and communicate openly with the bank about why you defaulted.

## 2. Start investigating with plenty of lead time.

It is best to start your investigations at least three months before your mortgage fixation comes up. If you wait until you get the renewal offer from your current bank, your only option will be to renegotiate with them.

## 3. Know what your mortgage options are.

You can be sure that the banks know what products are being offered by competing banks to foreign investors.

Having that knowledge in hand can help you determine whether you should try to negotiate at with your current lender or look for a new one.

The current mortgage options can change frequently, so it is best to discuss things with a mortgage broker who is familiar with the offers for foreigners.

It is also important to understand what refinancing at another bank will require of you in terms of time and hassle. Right now, all banks would require your personal presence at some point in the mortgage process. Is it worth your time and the cost of a trip to Czech Republic?

## 4. Negotiate hard if you opt to renew with your current provider.

The first rate you will be offered will not be the best. As a point of reference, over the last months we have helped our clients achieve an average discount of 1.2% from the bank's initial offer.

Good things to bring to the bank's attention when you are negotiating is if you have been a good and reliable payer, what competing banks are offering, and whether you intend to do further investing – meaning the potential of additional loans for them.

As well, you could possibly reduce your interest by paying down the mortgage below a certain percentage of loan to value (LTV). Normally you will be offered lower interest rates for LTVs under 70 or 75%.

*Chapter Thirty-six*

# FULFILLING YOUR TAX OBLIGATIONS

*P**lease note that tax regulations can change frequently, so please consult a tax adviser in Czech Republic for the latest information. The following information was valid at the point of writing in August 2015.*

Taxes are the biggest 'expenditure' in our life, so it is well worth taking the time to understand them and to determine how we can reduce the amount we pay.

There are really two topics for discussion regarding taxes related to a Czech investment property. The first is the *legal obligations* of an owner, whether an SRO or an individual. The second is: how can an investor maximize their return with *tax strategies?*

This chapter will look at the first topic, and the following chapter will look at the second topic.

First of all, the obligations differ depending on whether the property is owned by an SRO or an individual.

## COMMON (SRO AND INDIVIDUAL) TAX OBLIGATIONS

1. Tax returns for both an SRO and an individual are due by March 31st unless a registered tax adviser holds a power of attorney for them and this is lodged with the Financial Office. In such cases, the tax deadline can be extended to June 30.

   The fines for not filing a tax return when you legally should are 0.05% of the unpaid tax or 0.01% of the loss for each day of delay to a maximum of 5% of unpaid tax or loss. If the fine is lower than 500 CZK, they will not charge anything, while the maximum fine is 300,000 CZK. While fines in the past were rarely applied, now you will be sure to get a fine for a late filing.

2. There is a 4% real estate transfer tax payable on the sale price of a property or the valuation price of the property, whichever is higher. The valuation price is set by a State-approved valuer. **3.** Losses in a year can be carried forward five years to offset profit in future years.

## SRO TAX OBLIGATIONS

1. An SRO must file a tax return, regardless of whether any business has been done and regardless of whether a profit was made or not.

2. Net profit in an SRO is taxed at 19%.

3. Capital gains of a property minus expenses are subject to SRO corporate tax. There is no capital gains exemption, even after holding the property for more than five years.

4. Dividend withholding tax is 15%.

## INDIVIDUAL TAX OBLIGATIONS

1.  An individual is only required to submit a tax return if rent is collected from the property during that calendar year, even if they are a tax resident of another country.

2.  Net profit from rent collected is taxed at personal income tax levels.

3.  If a property is not your personal residence and is sold after five years, there is no tax on the capital gains. If it is sold before five years, the capital gains are taxed at personal income tax levels.

I'll be the first to admit that this chapter was a little dry and boring. However, the next one promises to be more interesting with tax strategies and tips that investors should take advantage of.

*Chapter Thirty-seven*

# LEVERAGING YOUR TAX STRATEGIES

*P*lease note that tax regulations can change frequently, so make sure you consult a tax adviser in Czech Republic for the latest information. The following information was valid at the point of writing in August 2015.

This chapter discusses ways an investor can maximize the tax advantages that property offers them.

### COMMON TAX STRATEGIES (SRO AND INDIVIDUAL)

*Note of caution on receipts.*

Czech accounting standards are quite strict and require originals of tax receipts. Also, invoiced expenses should always be in the name of the SRO, not in the name of the owner or director of the SRO.

### SRO TAX STRATEGIES

#### 1. Depreciation

You should be using depreciation as a tax deferral method if you have a net profit or expect to have a net profit within the next 5 years. Why do I say 5 years? That is because you can only carry losses forward for 5 years. At the sale of your property you will need to pay SRO profit tax on the net profit, which is the sale price minus the depreciated value of the property in your books.

If you do not have income which the depreciation is offsetting (i.e. your costs are more than your income) it can be better not to depreciate the property.

## 2. Small office expenses

It is possible to expense office space, computer equipment, mobile costs, etc. which are related to the management of your property.

## 3. Vehicle costs

An SRO can own a vehicle and claim part or all of its costs as an expense. When claiming all of your costs, you can chose to use a flat expense rate of 5000 CZK/month for gasoline and not have to prove your actual usage. In this case, there is no need to keep a log book of your actual kilometres driven. You can claim up to three vehicles with this flat rate but the vehicles are expected to be used *only* for business.

If you claim a percentage of your costs you need to keep a log book which tracks the business use of your vehicle versus personal use. This is an extreme pain and if you are using it mostly for personal use, it can totally offset the tax advantages.

Tip: A scooter also qualifies for the 5000 CZK/month flat gasoline deduction. Purchasing a used scooter for 20,000 CZK and using the flat 5000 CZK/month expensing can be a way to reduce taxes.

### 4. Food costs

Although food costs cannot be directly expensed, they can be entered in the accounting. The benefit is that you do not have to pay dividend withholding tax on these costs.

The food costs should be directly related to the business, so coffee or water for the office, or lunch with a business partner.

• • • • • • • • • • • • • • • • • • • • • • • • • • • • • • • •

## One client tries to add family shopping trips to accounting

*Tereza Lukuvkova, CZECH POINT 101's accountant said one client sent her 10 of his family shopping bills from grocery stores and wanted her to add these to his SRO accounts.*

*It is hard to prove how ketchup is required for you to operate a rental property.*

• • • • • • • • • • • • • • • • • • • • • • • • • • • • • • • •

*Notes of caution:*

### 1. Travel costs

If your 'sidlo' or SRO seat is registered in Prague, for example, and your rental property is in Prague, you cannot claim travel and accommodation expenses from the UK to Prague. These are viewed as normal obligations of travelling to the place of your work.

### 2. VAT registration

It is strongly discouraged to register for VAT only with the purpose of claiming VAT expenses related to a renovation. The Financial Offices frown upon an SRO registering for VAT but only collecting VAT, rather than also issuing invoices for VAT. This strategy has come back to bite some investors when the VAT was claimed back by the Financial Office along with interest and fines.

## INDIVIDUAL TAX STRATEGIES

### 1. Capital Gains Exemption

One of the biggest advantages of owning a property as a physical person rather than an SRO is that after holding the property for 5 years you do not have to pay any taxes on the capital gains.

### 2. Depreciation

Be sure you are using depreciation in your accounting. It can be used to offset income, thereby reducing the taxes you pay.

The good thing about depreciation is that you can use it to offset income but unlike with an SRO, after you have held the property for 5 years you do not have to pay any tax on the difference between the depreciated price in your accounting and your actual sale price.

### 3. Travel Costs

If your property is not where you live, or even if it is in the same city, you can claim travel costs and expenses related to the property.

For overseas investors this can include flight, hotel and car rental costs.

In all cases of travel costs, you need to be able to prove the purpose of the travel is related to the rental property, such as signing a contract at a Czech notary, etc.

*Notes of caution:*

### 1. Purchase costs

In order to claim expenses related to a purchase or immediately after a purchase (i.e. legal or real estate fees, furnishing costs, painting), you would need to collect rent from the property during that calendar year. Remember, losses on the books can be carried forward to offset income for up to 5 years.

### 2. Small office expenses

Although it is possible to expense small office expenses related to your property, such as office rental, computer equipment and mobile costs, you need to be very careful doing this. If you claim the whole cost of any of these items, you could be asked to prove that you have another one for personal use. It is possible to claim a percentage of the cost as related to managing your property.

• • • • • • • • • • • • • • • • • • • • • • • • • • • • • • • • • • •

## *Section Summary*

1. *95% of a successful rental is in finding a good tenant. Spend the time and effort up front to protect yourself from later problems.*

2. *A good tenant is to be valued. Treat them properly in order to keep them long term.*

3. *Don't accept the first offer from your bank when renewing a fixation period.*

4. *Small amounts saved in many areas can add up to a substantial amount. Try to manage your property as efficiently as possible.*

5. *Spend the time to figure out the best approach to your taxes. It will pay off in the long run!*

• • • • • • • • • • • • • • • • • • • • • • • • • • • • • • • • • • •

# THE SALE

*Chapter Thirty-eight*

# BID FAREWELL TO A POORLY PERFORMING PROPERTY

M any investors who bought at the peak of the Czech housing market with very high loan to value ratios grew tired
of carrying their properties through the recession. There is a
case to be made for a highly leveraged property when prices are
going up, but when they are flat or going down these properties
hang like an anvil around ones neck.

The purpose of this chapter is not to discuss whether buying
a cash flow negative property is a good idea, but rather to look at
possible exit paths for those who made this decision in the past.

There are two basic options: to sell or to abandon.

## SELL

To sell often requires that the investors must put in additional
money in order to completely pay off their mortgage and the
transfer tax.

There is nothing more painful when you have an open wound
than to rub salt in it. This is the situation faced by investors
who may have been supplementing their rent income for years

in order to cover the mortgage – in the hopes that prices would rebound – but now have decided they need to sell.

When evaluating the situation, an investor needs to go through the calculations based on the average costs of a sale.

Also, we always recommend assessing the investment *as it currently sits*. If you got some capital out, would you be able to get a better return in other investments after you factor in all the transaction costs?

If an investor wants to resell, but their early repayment penalty would make it unfeasible, it pays for them to have a frank discussion with their bank.

In some cases, banks become even more reasonable with the options once there have been a few months of default on the mortgage.

In fact, one bank that we were dealing with on behalf of a client frankly told us that the mortgage gets passed internally to a different department once there has been a few months of default. This department is given more power to adjust the terms of repayment and tends to be more flexible.

## ABANDON

I first must say that I personally in no way promote an investor trying to avoid obligations they have committed to. I am a strong believer that a person has a moral obligation to repay lenders they have borrowed money from.

However, many individuals have different feelings on the matter and this section will address some common questions they may have on this topic.

The most frequent is what a lender will do when a person abandons a property. We have been through this process with only one bank so this does not cover all possible scenarios with banks.

This bank's first step was to try to collect payment in any way possible, including passing it to an external collection agency. If this failed, they would then sell the debt to a third party at a reduction. This third party would then proceed with collecting the debt, either directly from the person or through execution on the property.

The execution process in Czech Republic is very long and protracted. It can cost the companies a considerable amount of money and at least a year of time to liquidate the property. They have the risk that the executer will not sell the property for the amount they need to make a profit since the executer is not obligated to sell it for a certain amount.

Because of this, the third party will sometimes contact the owner to ask them to transfer the property to them in exchange for a cancellation of the debt because it gives them an immediate return on their investment rather than having to take it through the courts.

Our experience has been that it is difficult but not impossible for the collection agencies to go after any assets that a defaulting owner has in another country. We have not seen this happen yet, but there are laws within the EU which make it possible.

The defaulting owner can be assured that if it is found out that they have other assets within Czech Republic, the company will also go after these.

The third party who bought the debt can also add substantial collection penalties to the amount of the debt purchased.

The defaulting owner can also be sure that they will be registered in the national database of debtors and be unable to borrow money for a substantial amount of time in Czech Republic.

*Chapter Thirty-nine*

# CALCULATING REALISTIC PROPERTY CLOSING COSTS

C alculating exit costs realistically is necessary for any Czech investor who is weighing the options of selling or keeping their property.

Let's look at the typical (and most probable) selling costs and also itemize additional costs when you own your property through an SRO.

### 1 Real estate fees or commission

Real estate fees or commission typically are from 3 to 5% (plus VAT) of the real estate sale price.

The fees are handled differently depending on where your property is located. In Brno the commission is typically added to the listed price and paid by the buyer. In almost all other locations including Prague, the real estate commission is within the listed price.

This fee can be negotiated!

## 2. Real estate transfer tax

The real estate transfer tax is currently at 4% of the sale price or valuation price, whichever is higher. The valuation must be done by a State-approved valuer.

## 3. Valuation by State-approved valuer

This depends on the size and location of your property but the typical cost for an apartment under 100 m2 ranges from 3,500 CZK to 7,500 CZK (plus VAT).

## 4. Redemption cost of the mortgage

If you pay the mortgage out on a day other than the exact date that your fixation comes up, you will need to pay a penalty for early repayment. This ranges from 5% to 25% of the unpaid amount of the mortgage.

These penalties are normally decided branch by branch so it is prudent to negotiate this *before* starting the sale process.

## 5. Final accounting and tax filing costs

The seller will need to file a real estate transfer tax form at the relevant Financial Office with both the sale contract and the valuation attached.

As well, if the property was owned by an SRO or an individual, they will need to file a tax return for the year in which they sold the property.

## 6. Income or corporate tax

If the property was owned by an individual and it was not held for a period of five years, there will need to be income tax paid on net profit from any capital gains.

An SRO will always need to pay corporate tax on the net profit from any capital gains.

If there is a net profit on the company and all shareholder loans have been repaid, there is also a dividend withholding tax that will need to be paid.

### 7. Possible additional costs

**a.** Escrow fees

A seller could also possibly have escrow costs from a notary, bank or attorney. Often this is paid entirely by the buyer but sometimes the agreement is made to split this cost.

**b.** Legal fees

You may choose to have an attorney check the escrow or contracts independent of the real estate agency. This is highly recommended as real estate agencies in Czech Republic are notorious for protecting only their own interests (i.e. their commission) and not the client's interests.

**c.** Power of Attorney representation

If you cannot physically be present to sign the purchase contract and turn over the apartment or utilities to the buyer, you will need to appoint someone with the power of attorney in order to represent you.

**d.** Liquidation or sale of your SRO

Anyone who purchased the SRO only for the purpose of holding the one property which is now sold, will have the painful cost of liquidating the company. The costs of liquidation are typically 50,000 to 75,000 CZK (+ VAT).

A preferable alternative is to find someone interested in a used company and give the company away for free.

**e.** Energy certificate

Stand-alone homes (but not those zoned for recreation) and individual flats which are being sold must obtain an energy certificate. This can only be provided by government authorized inspectors.

Apartment or flat owners should request an energy certificate from their association of owners. The association of owners needs to get one done for the entire building.

For a stand-alone home this can cost from 4,000 CZK to 10,000 CZK (plus VAT) depending on the size.

Here is a typical calculation on a flat sold for 3,000,000, including the real estate commission which was owned by an individual for more than 5 years (so no income tax payable). We are also assuming that the sale was timed to pay out the mortgage on the fixation date.

| Description | Amount (in CZK) |
| --- | --- |
| Sale price | 3,000,000 |
| Real estate fee (including VAT) | -180,000 |
| 4% real estate transfer tax | -120,000 |
| Cost of State-approved valuer (including VAT) | -7,200 |
| Concluding accounting and tax filing (including VAT) | -9,000 |
| Power of attorney representation for turnover (including VAT) | -4,800 |
| Miscellaneous items | -3,000 |
| Net amount for seller | **2,676,000** |
| Closing costs as a percentage of the sale price | **10.8%** |

*Chapter Forty*

# SQUEEZING MAXIMAL VALUE FROM YOUR PROPERTY AT RESALE

● ● ● ● ● ● ● ● ● ● ● ● ● ● ● ● ● ● ● ● ● ● ● ● ● ● ● ● ● ● ● ● ● ● ● ● ● ● ● ● ●

### *A good result: getting 42% above valuation*

*My wife and I sold three properties from 2009 to 2011.*

*We tried a few different methods to try to maximize our sale price. Some worked and some didn't.*

*When all was said and done and we analyzed the results, we noted that we had sold the properties for an average of 42% above valuations given by professionals.*

● ● ● ● ● ● ● ● ● ● ● ● ● ● ● ● ● ● ● ● ● ● ● ● ● ● ● ● ● ● ● ● ● ● ● ● ● ● ● ● ●

At the same time, we started using and testing these methods within our company. Here are some of the top things to do in a resale:

1   Investigate your mortgage payout options

All banks, at the time of this writing, have a penalty for early repayment of the mortgage. This can range from 5% to 25% of the unpaid amount of the mortgage.

Ouch!

With penalties like this, it would be investment suicide to sell a rental property at a time other than at the fixation point.

Just as a note for those who absolutely need to sell, the penalty can often be reduced through the individual branch that you deal with since they have the authority to be flexible on this.

Usually, the mortgage must be paid down on exactly the same day as it comes up for renewal, and the fact that you will be paying it down needs to be announced at least a month early.

As you can imagine, in order to hit the fixation date, the sale requires considerable planning and forethought.

2.   Satisfy legal requirements with regard to any tenants

A.   *Tenanted or empty?*

Because of the difficulty of evicting a non-paying tenant, a buyer who plans to personally live in the property will want to see it empty before signing the purchase contract. Or at least they will expect this before handover.

Even many investors will prefer to have it empty since they don't know if you are unloading the property because of a difficult tenant relationship.

B.    *Visits with prospective buyers*

Even if the contract specifically mentions that you are allowed to bring prospective buyers through with a reasonable notice period, the tenant can refuse you (and your guests) entry.

Most contracts include the statement that an owner can access the apartment in the case of an emergency, but are often missing a statement about viewings with prospective new tenants or buyers.

*Highly recommended:* Because of the above factors connected with a resale, as well as the other issues which are raised with a direct rent contract in Czech Republic (see chapter 28), we strongly recommend (and 99% of our property management clients use) a sub-rental contract system.

3.    Price your property correctly from the start

There are lots of opinions regarding pricing strategies, but the one that we have found most effective is to price slightly below the market valuation of your property. By slightly below, I am talking about 2 to 3%.

With the properties that my wife and I have personally resold, and more recently with some of our clients, we have found that this made the interested parties less inclined to haggle about the price. They realize it is a good deal and feel anxious to move forward quickly.

Another thing to keep in mind is: if your pricing is close to a rounded five hundred thousand or million, it is better to price it slightly under than slightly over. The reason is that so many people set thresholds in terms of how much they are willing to spend and it is usually in a rounded amount of five hundred thousand. This figure is also what they search with, so by dropping *below* a threshold you can get your advertisement seen by many, many more potential buyers.

4.  Advertise on 'for sale by owner' venues

A major factor to consider in the Czech real estate market, which is very different from most Western markets, is the volume of residential transactions which happen outside of real estate agents.

As mentioned in a previous chapter on finding an ideal property, a full 60% of residential real estate transactions are estimated to occur outside of real estate agents.

No doubt the lack of regulation is a major factor which has contributed to real estate agents having such a bad reputation. Some major real estate chains have recently entered the market and there is serious talk about a regulatory board, which would help improve the image of the profession. We can only hope.

At any rate, this is the fact of the matter right now, and a potential seller has to take this into consideration if they want to achieve the best possible result from their resale.

## Chapter Forty-one

# HOW TO DEAL WITH AN SRO USED FOR PROPERTY

M any foreign owners bought at a time when the use of an SRO (Czech limited liability company) was required by non-Czech citizens.

Almost always they are forced to sell the property from the SRO rather than being able to make a share transfer of the SRO.

This leaves them with an empty SRO that they need to take care of.

Surprise! Liquidating an SRO is just as expensive and bureaucratic as it was setting it up.

The liquidation process can take 6 to 8 months and require a lot of additional costs, sometimes as much as 100,000 CZK, including VAT, by the time you factor in the final accounting, the notarial deeds required and the cost of the executor.

Because of this, the best solution, and the one we always recommend, is for people to try and give their SRO away. There are foreigners who are looking for an SRO with a business history to be used either for a visa application or for an application for a loan at a bank.

An SRO owner can try websites like www.expats.cz, www. prague.tv or http://prague.craigslist.cz/ and offer to give the SRO away for free if the buyer pays for the transfer costs.

What can you do to make your SRO more attractive to a potential taker?

The first thing is that it's important to have your accounting up to date.

Secondly, you can get an absence-of-debt statement from the Financial Office, which, in Czech, is called a 'bezdlužnost'. Basically this confirms that from the point of the Financial Office, there are no outstanding debts which need to be paid.

## WHAT WILL HAPPEN TO MY SRO IF I ABANDON IT?

If the SRO is simply abandoned, what are the consequences?

After attempts to communicate with the owner of the company, the Commercial Court will appoint a liquidator who will proceed with the execution of the company. This is usually about 3 years after the abandonment of the company.

This can prove to be a problem for the owner of the property where the seat of the company is registered, as an executor can come to seize assets in the seat in order to pay outstanding debts. The owner can be required to prove to the executor, for example, that the furniture in the seat does not belong to the SRO.

If an owner has an abandoned SRO registered at their property, they can unilaterally file a document to the Commercial Court stating that the SRO no longer has permission to use their property. The registration will stay in the Commercial Court registry, but the Court will make efforts to contact the SRO owners regarding a new registered seat.

Additionally, the company will be entered in SOLUS, which is the national registry of debtors. At this point, we are not sure whether the owners would also be entered or only the company.

Anyone who is entered in this registry can have a very hard time ever getting a loan or lease, or even a mobile/internet contract, in Czech Republic.

• • • • • • • • • • • • • • • • • • • • • • • • • • • • • • • • • •

## *Section Summary*

**1.** *The costs of selling your property are currently around 10% of your sale price.*

2. *Investigate your mortgage payout options before putting your property up for sale. The banks usually have a prohibitive penalty on early repayment.*

3. *If your flat is tenanted, be sure that the proper contract is in place in order to meet your legal obligations to the tenant.*

4. *Advertise on 'for sale by owner' venues to reach the biggest audience.*

**5.** *Giving away a used and empty SRO for free is much cheaper than liquidating it.*

• • • • • • • • • • • • • • • • • • • • • • • • • • • • • • • • • •

# THE PARTS OF A LAND REGISTRY STATEMENT

**VÝPIS Z KATASTRU NEMOVITOSTÍ**
prokazující stav evidovaný k datu *15.03.2013 10:55:02*
Vlastnictví bytu a nebytového prostoru

*Vyhotoveno dálkovým přístupem do katastru nemovitostí pro účel ověření výstupu z informačního systému veřejné správy*
*ve smyslu § 9 zák. č. 365/2000 Sb., ve znění pozdějších předpisů.*

Okres: CZ0642 Brno-město      Obec: 582786 Brno

Kat.území: 611026 Komárov      List vlastnictví: 1600

V kat. území jsou pozemky vedeny v jedné číselné řadě

| A | Vlastník, jiný oprávněný | Identifikátor | Podíl |
|---|---|---|---|
| | Vlastnické právo | | |
| | CzechSky, s.r.o., náměstí Viléma Mrštíka 8, 66481 Ostrovačice | 26961351 | |

B *Nemovitosti*

*Jednotky*

| Č.p./ Č.jednotky | Způsob využití | Způsob ochrany | Podíl na společných částech domu a pozemku |
|---|---|---|---|
| 299/2 | byt | | 11990/40900 |
| | Budova Komárov, č.p. 299, LV 1599, bydlení | | |
| | na parcele | 249 | |
| | Parcely 249 | zastavěná plocha a nádvoří | 228m2 |
| 299/3 | byt | | 11990/40900 |
| | Budova Komárov, č.p. 299, LV 1599, bydlení | | |
| | na parcele | 249 | |
| | Parcely 249 | zastavěná plocha a nádvoří | 228m2 |
| 299/5 | byt | | 6935/40900 |
| | Budova Komárov, č.p. 299, LV 1599, bydlení | | |
| | na parcele | 249 | |
| | Parcely 249 | zastavěná plocha a nádvoří | 228m2 |
| 299/6 | garáž | | 1975/40900 |
| | Budova Komárov, č.p. 299, LV 1599, bydlení | | |
| | na parcele | 249 | |
| | Parcely 249 | zastavěná plocha a nádvoří | 228m2 |

B1 *Jiná práva -* **Bez zápisu**

C *Omezení vlastnického práva*

*Typ vztahu*
*Oprávnění pro*      *Povinnost k*

o **Zástavní právo smluvní**
  ve výši 5.525.000,- Kč (i k podílu na pozemku)

| **Raiffeisenbank a.s.,** Hvězdova | Jednotka: 299/3 | V-22915/2008-702 |
|---|---|---|
| 1716/2b, Nusle, 14078 Praha, | Jednotka: 299/2 | V-22915/2008-702 |
| RČ/IČO: 49240901 | | |

*Listina* Smlouva o zřízení zástavního práva podle obč.z. ze dne 27.04.2007. Právní účinky
  vkladu práva ke dni 30.04.2007.

                                                V-6453/2007-702

D *Jiné zápisy -* **Bez zápisu**

E *Nabývací tituly a jiné podklady zápisu*

*Listina*

Nemovitosti jsou v územním obvodu, ve kterém vykonává státní správu katastru nemovitostí ČR
Katastrální úřad pro Jihomoravský kraj, Katastrální pracoviště Brno-město, kód: 702.
strana 1

161

**VÝPIS Z KATASTRU NEMOVITOSTÍ**
prokazující stav evidovaný k datu 15.03.2013 10:55:02

*Vyhotoveno dálkovým přístupem do katastru nemovitostí pro účel ověření výstupu z informačního systému veřejné správy ve smyslu § 9 zák. č. 365/2000 Sb., ve znění pozdějších předpisů.*

Okres: CZ0642 Brno-město　　　　　　　　　　Obec: 582786 Brno

Kat.území: 611026 Komárov　　　　　　　　List vlastnictví: 1600

V kat. území jsou pozemky vedeny v jedné číselné řadě

---

*Listina*

○ Smlouva kupní  ze dne 14.05.2007. Právní účinky vkladu práva ke dni 14.05.2007.

　　　　　　　　　　　　　　　　　　　　　　V-7269/2007-702

　　*Pro:* CzechSky, s.r.o., náměstí Viléma Mrštíka 8, 66481 Ostrovačice  RČ/IČO: 26961351

○ Prohlášení vlastníka budovy o vymezení jednotek (zák.č.72/1994 Sb.)  ze dne 11.12.2008.
Právní účinky vkladu práva ke dni 12.12.2008.

　　　　　　　　　　　　　　　　　　　　　　V-22915/2008-702

　　*Pro:* CzechSky, s.r.o., náměstí Viléma Mrštíka 8, 66481 Ostrovačice  RČ/IČO: 26961351

---

F　　*Vztah bonitovaných půdně ekologických jednotek (BPEJ) k parcelám* - **Bez zápisu**

---

Upozornění: Další údaje o budově a pozemcích uvedených v části B jsou vždy na příslušném
　　　　　výpisu z katastru nemovitostí pro vlastnictví domu s byty a nebytovými
　　　　　prostory.

*Nemovitosti jsou v územním obvodu, ve kterém vykonává státní správu katastru nemovitostí ČR:*
**Katastrální úřad pro Jihomoravský kraj, Katastrální pracoviště Brno-město, kód: 702.**

*Vyhotovil:*　　　　　　　　　　　　　Vyhotoveno: 15.03.2013 11:03:09

*Český úřad zeměměřický a katastrální - SCD*

　　　Ověřuji pod pořadovým číslem V 209/2013, že tato listina, která
　　　vznikla převedením výstupu z informačního systému veřejné
　　　správy z elektronické podoby do podoby listinné, skládající
　　　se z ...Ž... listů, odpovídá výstupu z informačního systému
　　　veřejné správy v elektronické podobě.

　　　V ............... dne ...............

　　　Podpis ............... Razítko ...............

---

*Nemovitosti jsou v územním obvodu, ve kterém vykonává státní správu katastru nemovitostí ČR*
Katastrální úřad pro Jihomoravský kraj, Katastrální pracoviště Brno-město, kód: 702.
strana 2

A land registry statement has a headline and then section A, B, B1, C, D, E, F.

**The headline** shows the district, city, land registry territory, number of the land registry statement and title.

**A.**　　Contains details about the owners and/or co-owners and other rights. It identifies clearly the owners, shares on the common and other areas, as well as legal relationships.

*Practical use:* You can see if you are dealing with the correct owner or if there are multiple parties involved. In the above example, it is a company – CzechSky, SRO.

**B.** Contains details about the properties connected with the owners in section A. Here we can find:

- Land plots (parcel nbr., m2, type of land, zoning of the land (building/agricultural/forest...)

- Buildings (part of the town, building nbr., zoning of the building (family/rental/cottage...), parcel nbr.,

- Flats (building nbr., flat nbr., location of the flat, zoning of the flat (residential or commercial), share of the common areas, share of the land)

In this section you will find a note if there are any changes in process in the Land Registry. This will be indicated by a P which stands for Plomba (in Czech) or seal (in English)

*Practical use:* Using this, make sure that you are dealing with the correct piece of property. Also, by getting a copy of this issued before signing a purchase contract, you can check that there is not another sale already in process on the property. The above example gives four individual units – three flats and one garage.

**B1.** Contains rights to other properties connected with section B

*Practical use:* This could contain your right of access through another piece of land to access your property. (In the example, there is nothing listed.)

**C.** Contains any limitations on the ownership, whether pre-purchase rights, burdens, executions, liens associated with mortgages or loans, etc.

BEWARE: Some burdens do not have to be in the land registry statement and still could be valid. Also, based on decisions of the Supreme Court, the fact that a burden is deleted in the Land Registry does not mean that it does not exist.

*Practical use:* Find out if the seller has a mortgage, loans or other burdens on the property. These can indicate how motivated the seller might be, or they can mean a difficult sale process since liens have to be lifted before the property can be transferred. In the example, there is a mortgage listed for 5,525,000 CZK (which would have been the value when the liens were registered), and there are liens registered on units 2 and 3. If you find out that there is a lien or burden and the owner promises to delete this lien or burden during the purchase process, be sure to ask him to show you not only that it was deleted at the Land Registry, but also that the right for a lien has been actually ended or cancelled.

**D.**    Other entries – notes, records or other procedures.

**E.**    Contains title deeds and other docs.

*Practical use:* This section can show how the person obtained the property and when. How the seller obtained a property should be checked by your legal team in that they should get a copy of the purchase contract, inheritance rights, etc. In the example, the property was obtained by a purchase contract on 14.05.2007. Also, there is a statement from the owner regarding definition of the flats from 11.12.2008.

**F.**    Agricultural lands in section B, specified based on parcel nbr., code **BPEJ** and m2. BPEJ shows the quality of land and therefore its economic potential.

# BASIC CZECH EXPRESSIONS

| TERM | DEFINITION |
| --- | --- |
| Dobrý den | Literally 'Good day' |
| Těší mě | Nice to meet you |
| Na shledanou | Good-bye |
| Děkuji | Thank you |
| Ano | Yes |
| Ne | No |
| Jmenuji se... | My name is... |
| Nerosumín | I don't understand |

# COMMONLY USED CZECH REAL ESTATE TERMS

| Term | Definition |
|------|------------|
| 1+kk, 2+kk, 3+kk, etc. | The first number is the total number of rooms (including living room) and the '+kk' signifies that the kitchen/dining room are combined with the living room. Thus a '2+kk' is a one-bedroom apartment with the kitchen and dining room combined with the living room. |
| 1+1, 2+1, 3+1, etc. | As above, the first number is the total number of rooms but the '+1' in this case indicates that the kitchen is in a separate room. Thus a '3+1' is a two-bedroom apartment with living room and an additional room with the kitchen. |
| Osobní vlastnictví (OV) | Private ownership (please see the chapter 'Interpreting the different types of property ownership'). |
| Družstevní vlastnictví (DV) | Cooperative ownership (please see the chapter 'Interpreting the different types of property ownership'). |
| Cihlová | Built with brick or block construction. Buildings with this construction are the most sought after. |
| Panelová | Built with concrete panel construction. This construction typifies the buildings constructed during Communist times. |
| Jiné | Other construction. These have some other type of construction method. |
| Podlaží | Floor, as in which floor of an 8-story building the flat is on. |

| Plocha užitková | All usable living space connected with a property, including cellar space or balconies. |
|---|---|
| Plocha obytná (podlahová) | All usable living space connected with a property, not including cellar space or balconies. |
| Na prodej | For sale |
| Ložnice | Master bedroom |
| Obývací pokoj | Living room |
| Pokoj | Room |
| Koupelna | Bathroom, typically without the toilet. |
| WC | The room where the actual toilet is. |
| Chodba | Hallway |
| Šatna | Cloakroom |
| Komora | Pantry |
| Balkón | Balcony |
| Lodžie | Walled (typically with glass) but unheated balcony. |
| Terasa | Terrace – typically larger than a balcony and can be on ground level or on the roof of another part of the building. |
| Sklep | Cellar |
| Provize | Commission (in real estate, typically from the real estate). |
| Novostavba | New construction |
| Garáž | Garage |
| Cena | Price |
| Inkaso | Monthly payments, including fees paid to the association of owners as well as other costs such as electrical, water or gas. |
| Prohlídka | Viewing or tour of a property. |
| Výhled | The view (for example, from a window). |

# USEFUL LINKS – CZECH REPUBLIC SPECIFIC

| Link | Description |
|------|-------------|
| cuzk.cz | Online land registry |
| justice.cz | Online companies register |
| sreality.cz | Real estate for sale – mostly from real estate agents |
| bezrealitky.cz | Real estate for sale – direct from owners |
| czso.cz | Czech Statistical Office |
| nkcr.cz | Database of public notary offices |
| https://www.hypotecnibanka.cz/o-nas/pro-media/hb-index/ | Hypoteční banka's index of the actual sale price of property |
| realitymorava.cz/statistiky | Statistics on the average list prices (historical and current) for the major cities |
| hypoindex.cz | Tracking of mortgage rate offers from various banks |
| czechpoint101.com/investment-calculation | A spreadsheet with the fundamentals of assessing an investment property |

# USEFUL LINKS – PROPERTY INVESTMENT IN GENERAL

| Link | Description |
|------|-------------|
| canequity.com/mortgage-calculator/ | Mortgage calculator which shows not only monthly payments but amount of principal paid over time. |
| investopedia.com/calculator/cagr.aspx | Compound Annual Growth Rate calculator (CAGR) |

www.ingramcontent.com/pod-product-compliance
Lightning Source LLC
Chambersburg PA
CBHW072310210326
41519CB00057B/3806